SYNCHRONOUS PROGRAMMING OF REACTIVE SYSTEMS

THE KLUWER INTERNATIONAL SERIES
IN ENGINEERING AND COMPUTER SCIENCE

REAL-TIME SYSTEMS

Consulting Editor

John A. Stankovic

REAL-TIME UNIX SYSTEMS: *Design and Application Guide,*
B. Furht, D. Grostick, D. Gluch, G. Rabbat, J. Parker, M. McRoberts (eds.)
ISBN 0-7923-9099-7

FOUNDATIONS OF REAL-TIME COMPUTING: *Scheduling and Resource Management*, A. M. van Tilborg, G. M. Koob (eds.)
ISBN 0-7923-9166-7

FOUNDATIONS OF REAL-TIME COMPUTING: *Formal Specifications and Methods*, A. M. van Tilborg, G. M. Koob (eds.)
ISBN 0-7923-9167-5

REAL-TIME SYSTEMS ENGINEERING AND APPLICATIONS
M. Schiebe, S. Pferrer
ISBN 0-7923-9196-9

CONSTRUCTING PREDICTABLE REAL-TIME SYSTEMS
W. A. Halang, A. D. Stoyenko
ISBN 0-7923-9202-7

SYNCHRONIZATION IN REAL-TIME SYSTEMS: *A Priority Inheritance Approach*
R. Rajkumar
ISBN 0-7923-9211-6

SYNCHRONOUS PROGRAMMING OF REACTIVE SYSTEMS

by

Nicolas Halbwachs

IMAG Institute, Grenoble, France

Kluwer Academic Publishers
by Kluwer Academic Publishers,
101 Philip Drive, Norwell, MA 02061, U.S.A.

in all other countries, sold and distributed
by Kluwer Academic Publishers Group,

KLUWER ACADEMIC PUBLISHERS
DORDRECHT / BOSTON / LONDON

Library of Congress Cataloging-in-Publication Data

Halbwachs, Nicolas.
    Synchronous programming of reactive systems / by Nicolas
Halbwachs.
        p.   cm. -- (The Kluwer international series in engineering and
computer science ; 215)
    Includes bibliographical references (p.   ) and index.

    1. Real-time programming. 2. Programming languages (Electronic
computers)   I. Title. II. Series.
QA76.54.H36 1993
005.13--dc20   92-38480

ISBN 978-1-4419-5133-5

Published by Kluwer Academic Publishers,
P.O. Box 17, 3300 AA Dordrecht, The Netherlands.

Kluwer Academic Publishers incorporates
the publishing programmes of
D. Reidel, Martinus Nijhoff, Dr W. Junk and MTP Press.

Sold and distributed in the U.S.A. and Canada
by Kluwer Academic Publishers,
101 Philip Drive, Norwell, MA 02061, U.S.A.

In all other countries, sold and distributed
by Kluwer Academic Publishers Group,
P.O. Box 322, 3300 AH Dordrecht, The Netherlands.

Printed on acid-free paper

Contents

List of Figures

ix

List of Tables

Foreword

This book will attempt to give a first synthesis of recent works concerning reactive system design. The term "reactive system" has been introduced in order to avoid the ambiguities often associated with by the term "real-time system," which, although best known and more suggestive, has been given so many different meanings that it is almost inevitably misunderstood. Industrial process control systems, transportation control and supervision systems, signal-processing systems, are examples of the systems we have in mind.

Although these systems are more and more computerized, it is surprising to notice that the problem of time in computer science has been studied only recently by "pure" computer scientists. Until the early 1980s, time problems were regarded as the concern of performance evaluation, or of some (unjustly scorned) "industrial computer engineering," or, at best, of operating systems.

A second surprising fact, in contrast, is the growth of research concerning timed systems during the last decade. The handling of time has suddenly become a fundamental goal for most models of concurrency. In particular, Robin Milner's pioneering works about synchronous process algebras gave rise to a school of thought adopting the following abstract point of view: As soon as one admits that a system can instantaneously react to events, i.e., if the execution time of the machine is considered negligible with respect to the response delays of its environment, the time behavior of a system can be formalized in a very simple and elegant way.

The third surprise is that this synchronous point of view was applied to programming almost exclusively by French projects. Three projects started, quite independently, in the early 1980s, aiming at designing the three synchronous programming languages ESTEREL (ENSMP & INRIA), SIGNAL (INRIA/IRISA), and LUSTRE (IMAG). Other languages like SML, STATECHARTS, or L.0, which were developed in other countries, adopt some aspects of the synchronous model; but on the one hand, these languages do not thoroughly use this model, and on the other hand, they were not designed to be used for programming (SML is a hardware description language, STATECHARTS were designed as a specification lan-

*guage, and L.0 is a language for specifying communication protocols).
The three French groups rapidly noticed that their languages were based
on the same model. A tight cooperation was set up, that focused in particular on compiling methods and broadcasting the synchronous point of
view to the industrial world. This community was joined by another,
more recent project, concerning the language* ARGOS *(IMAG), a purely
synchronous variant of* STATECHARTS.

*This book is therefore a survey of very recent work, some of which
is still under development. Being myself strongly involved in the development of one of these languages — the language* LUSTRE *— I cannot
claim to give a fully unbiased presentation: it is often influenced by
my personal opinion and my present knowledge of the subjects. On the
other hand, several parts of this book have been partially borrowed from
existing papers devoted to each language. For their permission to borrow
this material, and for many helpful comments about the manuscript, I
would like to thank Gérard Berry, Albert Benveniste, Paul Caspi, Paul
Le Guernic, and Florence Maraninchi. I am also grateful to Corinne
Pichon, who carefully corrected the English version.*

*A first draft of this book (written in French) was used as lecture notes
for a 12-hour course given at the 21th AFCET International School of
Computer Science, held in San Sebastian (Spain) in July 1991.*

List of academic and industrial contacts concerning each language

Esterel:

- Gérard Berry, CMA/ENSMP, Sophia Antipolis - 06565 Valbonne, France

- Jean-Pierre Paris, CISI-Ingéniérie, Sophia Antipolis - 06565 Valbonne, France

- Philippe Couronné, ILOG S.A. , 2, Avenue Galiéni - 94253 Gentilly, France

Argos:

- Florence Maraninchi, IMAG, B.P. 53 - 38041 Grenoble, France

Lustre:

- Paul Caspi or Nicolas Halbwachs, IMAG, B.P. 53 - 38041 Grenoble, France

- Daniel Pilaud, VERILOG, ZAC du Pré Millet - 38330 Montbonnot, France

Signal:

- Albert Benveniste or Paul Le Guernic, IRISA/INRIA, Campus de Beaulieu - 35042 Rennes, France

- François Dupont, TNI, ZI du Vernis - 29608 Brest, France

Explanation of acronyms

ENSMP: *Ecole Nationale Supérieure des Mines de Paris*

INRIA: *Institut National de Recherche en Informatique et Automatique*

IRISA: *Institut de Recherche en Informatique et Systèmes Aléatoires*

IMAG: *Institut d'Informatique et de Mathématiques Appliquées de Grenoble*

Chapter 1

Introduction

1.1 Reactive systems

Reactive systems are computer systems that continuously react to their environment at a speed determined by this environment. This class of systems has been introduced [HP85, Ber89] in order to distinguish these systems, on the one hand, from *transformational* systems — i.e., classical systems, whose inputs are available at the beginning of the execution and which deliver their outputs when terminating — and, on the other hand, from *interactive* systems, which continuously interact with their environment, but at their own rate (e.g., operating systems). Most industrial "real-time" systems are reactive — control, supervision and signal-processing systems — but other examples concern communication protocols or man-machine interfaces.

The main features of these systems are the following:

They involve concurrency: At the least, the concurrency between the system and its environment must be taken into account. Moreover, it is often convenient and natural to consider such a system as made of a set of parallel components, that cooperate to achieve the intended behavior. Finally, these systems are sometimes implemented on parallel or distributed architectures in order to increase their performances or their reliability. However, let us note that the logical decomposition of a system into parallel processes generally has nothing to do with an actual

1

concurrent implementation, and, even if such a concurrent implementation is performed, the physical decomposition is not necessarily the same as the logical one. There is no reason for a logical decomposition of a problem into subproblems to satisfactorily meet performance or fault tolerance criteria on a given architecture.

They are submitted to strict time requirements: These requirements concern both their input rate and their input/output response time. These constraints must be expressed in the system specifications, they must be taken into account during the system design, and their satisfaction must be checked on the implementation. Time-constraint fulfillment obviously requires efficient implementation, but it especially necessitates precise evaluation of execution time.

They are generally deterministic: The outputs of such a system are entirely determined by their input values and by the occurrence times of these inputs. This determinism distinguishes reactive systems from interactive ones: most interactive systems are intrinsically nondeterminist. An operating system contains, for instance, schedulers that dynamically activate and interrupt processes according to various parameters (CPU load, resource availability, priorities, ...). The result of a call to the system generally depends on these parameters. The design, analysis, and debugging of a deterministic system are much easier. So the inherent determinism of reactive-system specifications must be preserved in their implementation.

Their reliability is an especially important goal: This may be their most important feature. It is a commonplace to say that errors in reactive systems can have dramatic consequences, involving human lives and huge amount of money. The economic and human consequences of an error in the software driving a satellite or controlling a nuclear plant can obviously be incalculable. Therefore, these systems require especially rigorous design methods and constitute a field where formal verification must be considered.

Generally, they are made partly by software and partly by hardware: Many reactive systems are still implemented by hardware, for reasons of cost or performance or for historical reasons. In many other cases, they are partly implemented by hardware, and the hardware and software parts are separated quite late during the design.

1.2 Classical approaches

As noted above, reactive systems have been for a long time (and often still are) implemented by hardware (analog machines, switch systems, and custom circuits). When implemented by software, they are often programmed in assembly language for efficiency purposes. At a higher level, "operating system" approaches (real-time monitors) or general-purpose parallel languages are used. Models include automata or Petri-net-based models, task-based models, and communicating processes.

Deterministic automata: Automata are often used to implement the control kernel of a reactive system. Given a set of input values, the automaton selects a transition from its current state, calls the corresponding sequential tasks, and changes its state for its next reaction. Such an approach generally leads to excellent and measurable performances; a reaction is a "linear" piece of code (neither loop nor recursivity, no interrupt, no overhead due to process management), whose maximal execution time can be accurately bounded. Moreover, automata are well-known mathematical objects for which verification techniques are available (evaluation of temporal logic formulas [CES86, QS82], reduction and observation [Ver86, Fer90]).

However, automata are "flat" objects, without any hierarchical or parallel structure. Consequently, they are very difficult to use to design complex systems. Writing an automaton with about ten states only is a difficult and error-prone task. The slightest modification in the system specifications may involve a complete modification and rewriting of the automaton.

Petri-net-based models: These models are mainly used to program industrial controllers. The inherent concurrency of these models reduces the complexity of system description. However, because of the lack of hierarchy, they are hard to apply to big systems. Moreover, their semantics, especially concerning time aspects, is often unclear.

Task-based models: Here, we mean the approach consisting in designing a system as made of a set of sequential tasks, activated and controlled by a real-time operating system. The system is decomposed into tasks that generally communicate with each other by means of a shared memory. In our opinion, this is a low-level approach. Time constraints are not directly expressed in the description; they can only be satisfied by means of scheduling instructions (interrupts, priorities, ...) given to the operating system. Program portability is doubtful. System analysis is made difficult because of nondeterminism and lack of a global view. Performances can deteriorate because of tasks management and dynamic scheduling.

Communicating processes: General-purpose parallel languages, such as ADA [ADA83] or OCCAM [INM84] are on a higher level. These languages offer high-level primitives to structure programs and data. Communication and synchronization mechanisms (rendezvous, fifo queues, ...) are much cleaner than shared memory. These languages have been designed in order to increase program portability. However, this portability is achieved at the expense of nondeterminism. For a program behavior to be independent of the target architecture (mono- or multiprocessor), only minimal assumptions are made about inter-process synchronization. Even if some of these languages have been provided with "real-time" primitives, the semantics of these primitives is generally vague. We illustrate these problems by means of a classical example of an ADA program, where a task A signals "minutes" to a task B, by counting "seconds":

```
loop
delay 60; B.MINUTE
end
```

This program does not provide the intended behavior: for a MINUTE to be received by B, A must have been waiting for 60 seconds, but B must also listen to it, and, moreover, the rendezvous must take place — and the occurrence time of this rendezvous is left unspecified in the language semantics. The delay separating two successive receptions of MINUTE is *at least* 60 seconds. On the other hand, a signal cannot be broadcast: if A must send MINUTE to a third task C, A must also execute C.MINUTE. B and C will *never* receive MINUTE at the same time. In such a language, different processes never have the same view of the global state of the program. The last drawback of general-purpose parallel languages for real-time programming is the tremendous overhead that can be involved by runtime process management.

As a conclusion to this brief overview of classical tools to reactive system design, let us notice that the user must choose between determinism and concurrency. All parallel languages are based on asynchronous execution schemes, where processes compete with each other for resources, and where this competition is nondeterministically solved. Synchronous languages may be viewed as an attempt to reconcile concurrency and determinism.

1.3 The synchronous approach

Synchronous languages have been designed to make the programmer's task easier, by providing him with "ideal" primitives, which allow a program to be considered as *instantaneously* reacting to external events. Each internal or output event of the program is precisely dated with respect to the flow of input events. The behavior of a program is fully deterministic, both from the functional and from the time point of view.

In fact, the notion of physical (chronometric) time is replaced by a simple notion of order among events: the only relevant notions are the simultaneity and precedence between events. Physical time does not play any special role (as it does in ADA); it will be handled as an external event, exactly as any other event coming from the program environment. This is called the *multiform notion of time*. As an example, let us consider the two following requirements:

"The train must stop within 10 seconds"
and
"The train must stop within 100 meters"

Conceptually, these two constraints are of the same nature. However, in a language where physical time (counted in "seconds") plays a particular role and is handled by special statements, they will be expressed in completely different ways. In the synchronous model, they will be expressed by similar precedence constraints:

"The event *stop* must precede the 10th (respectively, 100th)
next occurrence of the event *second* (respectively, *meter*)"

When we will speak of *an instant*, this notion will be understood as a
logical instant: the history of a system is a totally ordered sequence of
logical instants; at each of these instants, zero, one, or several events
occur. Event occurrences that happen at the same logical instant are
considered simultaneous; those that happen at different instants are ordered as their instants of occurrence. Apart from these logical instants,
nothing happens either in the system or in its environment. Finally,
all the processes of the system have the same knowledge of the events
occurring at a given instant.

In practice, the synchrony hypothesis is the assumption that the
program reacts rapidly enough to perceive all the external events in
suitable order. If this assumption is satisfied — and, more importantly,
if its satisfaction can be checked — the synchronous hypothesis is rather
a more realistic abstraction than the one that consists in considering
that a machine deals with "actual" integer or real numbers. Moreover,
we will see that synchronous languages can be implemented in a particularly efficient and *measurable* way. The object code is structured as a
finite automaton, a transition of which corresponds to a reaction of the
program. As noted before, the code corresponding to such a transition
is linear (loop-free), and its maximal execution time can be accurately
bounded on a given machine. Therefore, the validity of the synchrony
hypothesis can be checked.

1.4   Complex systems

However, synchronous languages do not pretend to solve all the problems raised by the design of real-time systems. A real-life complex
system generally involves the cooperation of the three types of programs: for instance, a programmer makes use of a reactive interface
(keyboard, mouse, scrollbar) to call interactive services of the operating system and to activate transformational tasks. Generally speaking,
following [BG88], we can distinguish three parts in a complex real-time
system:

- A generally interactive *interface* with the environment, which acquires the inputs and processes the outputs. This level includes interrupt management, input reading from sensors, and conversion between logical and physical inputs/outputs. This level can also deal with the communication between several loosely coupled, synchronous components.

- One or more *reactive kernels*. Such a kernel computes the outputs from the logical inputs, by selecting the suitable reaction (computations and output emissions) to incoming inputs.

- A level of *data management*, which performs transformational tasks under the control of the reactive kernel.

This book essentially deals with reactive kernel design, which is the most specific and probably the most difficult part of the design of a complex real-time system. One must keep in mind, however, that these kernels are intended to be merged into more complex systems. As a consequence, synchronous languages are not complete languages. In particular, they do not offer primitives to define and handle complex data structures, which are left to a classical language (host language). Moreover, synchronous language compilers produce their object code in the host language, for this code will later on be integrated into a larger program.

1.5 Summary of this book

We will present the work concerning four languages: ESTEREL, ARGOS, LUSTRE, and SIGNAL. Rather than describing successively the parts concerning each of them, we prefer to sort them according to some general topics:

- Part I of this book presents each language, together with illustrating examples of programs. Examples have been chosen in order to highlight the most specific features of each language.

- Part II deals with compilation. We will successively present:

- nonclassical static verifications performed by compilers: causality checking in ESTEREL (§5.1) and ARGOS (§5.2), clock checking in LUSTRE, (§5.3) and clock synthesis in SIGNAL (§5.4).

- sequential code generation from ESTEREL (§6.1) and LUSTRE (§6.2) programs. ESTEREL and LUSTRE compilers share an original method to synthesize the control structure of the object code as a finite automaton. Both compilers generate the code in a common format, called OC (for "object code"), on which several tools can be applied (§6.3).

- distributed code generation. Two very different approaches will be presented. The first one has been applied to SIGNAL and makes use of the logical concurrency expressed in the source program. The second approach has been developed for LUSTRE, but can be applied to any language compiled towards OC, since it requires first the generation of sequential code.

- silicon compiling, from ESTEREL and LUSTRE (Chapter 8).

• Part III is devoted to program verification. The language LUSTRE itself can be used to express properties about programs (Chapter 9); these properties are checked by an exhaustive analysis of the automaton built by the compiler. Another approach, used to verify ESTEREL programs (Chapter 10), consists of reducing the generated automaton according to various suitable observation criteria.

Part I

Four Synchronous Languages

Chapter 2

The imperative language Esterel

2.1 Introduction

Among the languages we will present, ESTEREL is the oldest, since its design started in the early 1980s. It was developed in Gérard Berry's group and is a common project of INRIA and ENSMP in Sophia-Antipolis.

ESTEREL is an imperative, textual language, and its syntax is close to usual parallel languages. Paradoxically, because of this apparent analogy with classical languages, ESTEREL will be the best language to highlight the specificity of the synchronous approach. The formalization of fundamental concepts of synchronous programming is mainly a consequence of the design of ESTEREL, and the method to compile synchronous programs into automata was first proposed in the ESTEREL compiler. Today, ESTEREL is a commercial product (sold and maintained by two French software companies: CISI-Ingenierie and Ilog) that is actually used in the industry. The following overview of the language is essentially derived from [BCG87, BCG88].

2.2 Basic concepts

An ESTEREL program communicates with its environment by means of *signals* and *sensors*. Signals are used both as inputs and outputs, while sensors are used only as inputs. Signals can convey values; sensors always do. For instance, a train controller can receive a signal every millisecond, a signal every wheel revolution, track signals conveying positional informations, and signals coming from the operator keyboard; it can use sensors to measure the external temperature; it can emit power commands to the engines and brakes. It can be made of submodules, communicating with each other by means of internal signals.

Signals and sensors are identified by names. The notation S(v) expresses that the signal S conveys the value v.

Signals are broadcast among all the processes (though this broadcasting may be limited by scope rules; see below). When a signal is emitted (either by the environment or by an internal process), it is *instantaneously* perceived by all the processes that listen to it. One can think of programs as communicating via radio waves, each signal being represented by a frequency. Two kinds of information are broadcast on the waves: *values*, which are permanent, and *signal tops*, which are transient (they cannot be perceived by processes that do not listen to the signal when it occurs). A sensor has a value but no signal top. A *pure signal* has a signal top but no value. A *valued signal* has both, and a value change is always synchronous with a signal top (hence, the signal top is used to broadcast and detect value changes; there is no way to detect sensor value changes).

Values conveyed by signals can appear in expressions: if S is the name of a valued signal or of a sensor, ?S denotes its current value. A signal top is a control information that is handled by special control statements.

In ESTEREL, control takes no time. The occurrence of an input signal can instantaneously result in the emission of other signals. As a consequence, the following program fragment

```
every 60 SECOND do
   emit MINUTE
end
```

precisely emits the signal MINUTE every 60 occurrences of the signal SECOND. The emission of MINUTE is simultaneous with the 60th occurrence of SECOND.

This notion of simultaneity is captured by the concept of *event*. An event is a set of simultaneous occurrences of (possibly valued) signals. A particular run of a program is a sequence of events, called a *history*. We give below a possible history of a speed counter, receiving two signals SECOND and METER, and computing the valued signal SPEED every second:

{METER} , {SECOND,SPEED(1)} , {METER} , {METER,SECOND,SPEED(2)} , ...

There is a special built-in pure signal named tick that implicitly belongs to any event. In other words, tick occurs at any reaction of the program.

The same signal may be emitted several times at the same instant (e.g., by several processes). If such a signal is pure, the result is only that the signal is present in the current event. If it is a valued signal, it can be associated a "combination operator," noted by $*$: the result of the simultaneous emission of $S(v_1), S(v_2), ..., S(v_n)$ is then the occurrence of $S(v_1 * v_2 * \cdots * v_n)$ in the current event. As an example of the use of this combination mechanism, in ETHERNET-like local networks, signal broadcasting is physically realized on a cable. A special value NAK represents the collision of two messages. One sets $v_1 * v_2 =$ NAK for all v_1, v_2.

2.3   Programming primitives

The basic programming unit is the *module*, which contains a *declaration part* and a *statement part*.

Like all the synchronous languages considered here, ESTEREL is not a complete language. Data types, constants, functions, and procedures can be imported from a host language and are only declared as abstract names in the declaration part. Only a minimal set of types, constants, and operators are built in (integers, Boolean, usual arithmetic and logic operators).

2.3.1   Declarations

In the declaration part, we declare the types, constants, functions, and procedures used by the module (and defined in the host language); we then declare the signals and the sensors that define the module's interface. Finally, the declaration part may also include "relations," which are implication and exclusion relations among input signals; these are known properties of the environment, which are indicated to the compiler for optimization purposes. Here is a possible declaration part of a TIMER module, as it appears in the digital watch program described in [Ber91b]:

```
module TIMER
type TIME;
constant INITIAL_TIME : TIME ;
procedure INCREMENT_TIME (TIME) () ;
input  SECOND, RESET;
output TIMER_VALUE (TIME),
       BEEP (combine integer with PLUS);
relation SECOND # RESET ;
```

The procedure INCREMENT_TIME is declared with two lists of types: the first list types arguments passed by reference, and the second list types arguments passed by value (it is empty here). The output signal TIMER_VALUE conveys a value of type TIME and has no combination operator: its multiple emission is forbidden (it will be checked by the compiler). The multiple emission of the output signal BEEP is allowed: the integer values conveyed will then be added. Intuitively, several components of a watch can operate the beeper: the chime beeps once a second, the stopwatch beeps twice a second, and the alarm beeps four times a second. If some of these components beep together, the beep frequencies must be added. Finally, the given relation indicates that signals SECOND and RESET never occur at the same time (the # operator denotes exclusivity).

2.3.2   Expressions

The expressions are classically built from variables, constants, signal and sensor values (?S), and function calls.

2.3.3   Statements

There are two kinds of statements: *primitive* statements and *derived*
statements, which are defined in terms of primitive statements. The
primitive statements are themselves divided into two groups: classical
basic imperative statements, and temporal statements that deal with
signals.

Basic imperative statements

Here is the list of the basic imperative statements:

`nothing`	dummy statement
`halt`	halting statement
`<var> := <expression>`	assignment
`call <id> (<var_list>)(<exp_list>)`	external procedure call
`<stat>;<stat>`	sequence
`if <exp> then <stat>`	
`        else <stat> end`	conditional
`loop <stat> end`	infinite loop
`<stat> || <stat>`	parallel statement
`trap <id> in <stat>`	trap definition
`exit <id>`	exit from trap
`var <var_decls> in <stat> end`	local variable declaration
`signal <signal_decls>`	
`      in <stat> end`	local signal declaration
`run <name> <renaming>`	module instanciation

There are no shared variables: if a variable is updated in one
branch of a parallel statement, it cannot be read or written in the other
branches.

Remember that the execution machine is *infinitely fast*. The only
statement that takes time is the `halt` statement, which does nothing
and never terminates.[1] Therefore, `nothing` does nothing *in no time*,
assignment and external procedure calls are instantaneous, the second
statement of a sequence is started exactly when the first statement ter-

---

[1]We will see later that the infinite execution of a `halt` statement can be interrupted.

minates, and the branches of a parallel statement start simultaneously; a parallel statement terminates synchronously with the last termination of its branches. Hence, when a parallel statement is started, its branches work in the same signal environment.

The **trap-exit** mechanism is a classical escape mechanism: a **trap** defines a block that is instantly exited when a corresponding **exit** statement is executed. If several nested blocks are simultaneously exited, the effect is to instantly exit the outermost one. This mechanism is perhaps the most powerful control mechanism in ESTEREL. It extends to general exception facility.

The **run** statement allows module reuse. Its effect is a copy in place of the code of the module whose name is given. Some input/output signals can be renamed (by default, they are not). We will see later some examples of use of this statement.

Although statements are simultaneously executed, they are executed *in the right order*. Hence, a sequence

        X := 0 ; X := X+1

instantly yields **X=1**. Only finitely many statements can be executed simultaneously. One imposes a statically checked finiteness constraint to forbid loops like

        X := 0 ; loop X := X+1 end

Temporal statements and signal handling

All statements described so far "take no time," except **halt**. We now describe *temporal statements* that handle signals and can take time.

The signals can be either emitted by the program's environment or by the program itself. To emit a signal S conveying the value of an expression **<exp>**, one writes

        emit S(<exp>)

or simply "**emit S**" if S is a pure signal. An emission is instantaneous. If several emissions occur simultaneously, the values are combined, as described on page 13.

For signal reception, there are two primitive statements. The first tests for the presence of a signal in the current event:

> present S then <statement1> else <statement2> end

or, for a valued signal,

> present S(X) then <statement1> else <statement2> end

The semantics is clear: if S is present in the current event, then <statement1> is instantly started. Otherwise, <statement2> is instantly started. In the case of a valued signal, if the signal is present, the variable X instantly takes the value conveyed by the signal.

The second statement is the most important ESTEREL construct. It is called the *watchdog* and has the form

> do
> <statement>
> watching <occ>

where <statement> is any statement and where <occ> is an *occurrence* of a signal. An occurrence is either a signal name (e.g., SECOND) possibly preceded by the keyword **immediate,** or a signal name preceded by a count factor (e.g., 3 SECOND). This statement defines a time limit for the execution of its body. The time limit is defined by the occurrence <occ>. If <occ> has the form S (respectively, **immediate** S), the time limit is the first event in the strict future of the current event (respectively, in the future, including the current event) that contains an occurrence of the signal S. Similarly, for an occurrence n S, the time limit is the nth event in the strict future to contain S.

The body <statement> is started simultaneously with the watching statement (except if <occ> has the form **immediate** S and if S is present). It is executed up to the time limit *excluded*:

- If the body terminates strictly before the limit, the whole watching statement terminates synchronously;

- If the body is not terminated when the limit occurs, the body is instantly killed — *without being executed at that time* — and the watching statement terminates.

Notice that the nesting of **watching** statements establishes a natural preemption priority. Consider the following example:

```
do
    do
        <statement1>
    watching S1;
    <statement2>
watching S2
```

If S1 and S2 occur simultaneously, then the outermost **watching** statement is terminated, and `<statement2>` is not executed. Hence S2 preempts a simultaneous S1.

Let us also notice that we have now two basic ways to kill a statement `<stat>` on the occurrence of a signal S:

- the interrupt do `<stat>` **watching** S, and

- the withdrawal[2]

```
trap T in
        <stat>; exit T
    ||
        await S; exit T
end
```

The difference is that in the first case, when S occurs, the statement `<stat>` is not executed at that time (the interruption precedes the reaction), whereas in the second case, `<stat>` reacts before being killed (it can express its last wishes!).

Derived statements

Many useful temporal statements can be derived from primitive ones. For instance, one writes

```
                                        do
    await <occ>      instead of           halt
                                        watching <occ>
```

and

---

[2] see the definition of the **await** statement in the next section

```
    do                              do
      <stat>        instead of        <stat>; halt
    upto <occ>                      watching <occ>
```

The **await** statement has its intuitive meaning: it does nothing and terminates as soon as the awaited occurrence <occ> happens. Notice that many "real-time" languages offer such a statement (often with less precise semantics) as a primitive. However, though **await** can be derived from the **watching** statement, the converse is not true. So, the **watching** statement is more primitive and powerful. The difference between the upto and the **watching** statements is that "do <stat> upto <occ>" does not terminate when its body does, but always waits for <occ>. The **watching** statement could have been derived from the upto by writing

```
    trap T in
      do
        <stat>; exit T      instead of        do
      upto S                                     <stat>
    end                                        watching S
```

It is often useful to add a *timeout* clause to a watchdog; this clause is executed if the time limit occurs before termination of the body. We will then write

```
    do                                       trap T in
      <stat1>                                  do
    watching<occ>                                <stat1> ; exit T
    timeout            instead of              watching <occ>;
      <stat2>                                    <stat2>
    end                                        end
```

If <stat1> terminates strictly before <occ>, the block "trap" is instantly exited, and the timeout clause <stat2> is ignored.

Guarded loops are often used, by writing

```
                                             loop
    loop                                       do
      <stat>          instead of                 <stat>
    each 3 METER                               upto 3 METER
                                             end
```

and

```
      every 5 SECOND do                          await 5 SECOND;
          <stat>                instead of       loop
      end                                            <stat>
                                                 each 5 SECOND
```

In a "loop ... each <occ>" statement, the body starts immediately and
is restarted on every occurrence of <occ>; an "every <occ> do ..."
first waits for the first occurrence of <occ>.

Multiple waiting of signals is written

```
      await
          case <occ1> do <stat1>
          case <occ2> do <stat2>
          ...
          case <occn> do <statn>
      end
```

Unlike similar statements in asynchronous languages, this selection is
deterministic: the first occurrence determines the statement to be executed. If several occurrences simultaneously happen, the statement corresponding to the first such occurrence in the list is selected (therefore,
the order in the list establishes a priority relation between simultaneous
occurrences). The expansion of the multiple waiting is of the form

```
      do
          do
              ...
                  do
                      halt
                  watching <occn>
                  timeout <statn> end
              ...
          watching <occ2>
          timeout <stat2> end
      watching <occ1>
      timeout <stat1> end
```

A last useful derived statement allows the emission of a signal *at each
program reaction*. It makes use of the predefined "always present signal"
tick (cf. page 13). One can write

```
                                        loop
   sustain S         instead of          emit S
                                        each tick
```

2.4 Programming style and first examples

Before giving some examples, we illustrate some specific aspects of
ESTEREL programming: the use of several time scales, the use of signal
broadcasting, and simultaneity.

2.4.1 Using signals as time units

The multiform-time point of view, generally adopted in synchronous
programming, has been described before. In ESTEREL, this point of
view consists in using any signal as a "time unit" to count "delays."
An illustrating example appears in the "reflex game," which will be
treated later (§2.6). The core of the system must satisfy the following
specification:

> *Wait for a hit on a* READY *button within a time limit of*
> 10 SECOND; *in case of timeout, emit an* ALARM; *while waiting,*
> *any hit on the* STOP *button should ring a* BELL.

The corresponding program could be

```
   do
      do
         every STOP do emit RING_BELL end
      upto READY
   watching 10 SECOND
   timeout emit ALARM end
```

(Here "upto READY" is equivalent to "watching READY;" we prefer using
upto whenever we are not interested in the termination of the body)

Let us now consider the following specification:

> *Wait for* 10 SECOND; *if* STOP *is hit during that time, termi-*
> *nate and emit an* ALARM; *while waiting, any hit on* READY
> *should ring the* BELL.

This leads to the following program:

```
do
    do
        every READY do emit RING_BELL end
        upto 10 SECOND
    watching STOP
    timeout emit ALARM end
```

In some sense, this program appears to be *dual* to the first one; it can be read as

> *Wait for* 10 SECOND *within a time limit of* STOP; *in case of timeout, emit an* ALARM; *while waiting* ...

This symmetry comes from the fact that all signals play a similar role. The symmetry would completely disappear in a language like ADA, where the "real-time" (counted in seconds) plays a particular role and is handled by specific statements.

2.4.2   Use of broadcasting

Broadcasting simplifies process communication and improves modularity; when a process emits a signal, it does not need to know who is listening to that signal; conversely, when a process receives a signal, it does not need to know the emitter(s).

We illustrate this with the wristwatch example described in detail in [Ber91b]. A wristwatch is an excellent example of a reactive system; it is relatively small, but surprisingly complex, and has many features encountered in other systems: folding numerous commands into few buttons by using *command modes*, showing numerous data in few displays using *display modes*, and establishing communications and instantaneous dialogues between submodules. The wristwatch has five submodules: a WATCH that acts as a regular timekeeper, a STOPWATCH, an ALARM, a BUTTON_INTERPRETER that interprets wristwatch buttons as commands directed to the other modules according to the current command mode, and a DISPLAY_HANDLER that handles the various displays. Broadcasting makes life easier in several places:

- The external signal SECOND is automatically broadcast to all the modules that need it.

- Hitting a particular button in a particular mode provokes the toggling from 24H to AM/PM time display mode. This change concerns the watch and the alarm. The button interpreter broadcasts a message TOGGLE_24H_MODE_COMMAND without worrying about who is expecting this message. Adding a second alarm would not modify the corresponding code.

- The timekeeper broadcasts a WATCH_TIME signal whenever its internal time changes. This signal is used by both the alarm and the display handler. Adding a second alarm can be done without any modification of the WATCH and ALARM modules.

2.4.3　Instantaneous dialogue

The synchrony hypothesis allows a new form of communication, the *instantaneous dialogue*. A typical example appears in the wristwatch code, more precisely in the body of the stopwatch; it will be abstracted here. An instantaneous dialogue can be used whenever the behavior of a process P depends on some property of the internal state of another process Q. For simplification, assume that Q is a flip-flop on some signal FLIP_FLOP_COMMAND and that P must perform <stat1> if Q is in the "flip" state and <stat2> otherwise. Then we introduce two signals ARE_YOU_FLIP and I_AM_FLIP and writes Q as follows:

```
loop
    do
        loop
            emit I_AM_FLIP
        each ARE_YOU_FLIP
    ||
        <flip state code>
    upto FLIP_FLOP_COMMAND;
    do
        <flop state code>
    upto FLIP_FLOP_COMMAND
end
```

Now, the intended behavior of P is ensured by the following code:

```
emit ARE_YOU_FLIP
present I_AM_FLIP then
    <stat1>
else
    <stat2>
end
```

This example has been given to show the power of the assumption of simultaneity. However, instantaneous dialogues can often be avoided by using the sustain statement (tick and sustain were introduced late in the design of ESTEREL). A simpler solution of the above example could be

```
% Code for Q                          % Code for P
loop                                  present I_AM_FLIP then
    do                                    <stat1>
            sustain I_AM_FLIP         else
       ||                                 <stat2>
            <flip state code>         end
    upto FLIP_FLOP_COMMAND;
    do
        <flop state code>
    upto FLIP_FLOP_COMMAND
end
```

Another way to avoid instantaneous dialogue is to use Boolean-valued signals: whenever Q enters its "flip" state, it emits FLIP(true); whenever it enters the "flop" state, it emits FLIP(false). Then P only has to check ?FLIP to know the state of Q:

```
% Code for Q                          % Code for P
loop                                  if ?FLIP then
    emit FLIP(true);                      <stat1>
    do <flip state code>             else
    upto FLIP_FLOP_COMMAND;              <stat2>
    emit FLIP(false);                 end
    do <flop state code>
    upto FLIP_FLOP_COMMAND
end
```

All these solutions behave in exactly the same way, although the code generated for the last one may be slightly less efficient, since a part of the program control is hidden in a Boolean value (see §6.1).

2.4.4   A stopwatch

Let us write an ESTEREL program implementing the stopwatch of the digital watch presented in [Ber91b]. We will successively consider several versions, highlighting the language modularity: each version will be built from the previous version.

Simple stopwatch

The basic stopwatch receives an input signal START_STOP that alternatively puts it in "running" and "stopped" states. Initially the stopwatch is stopped. It also receives a signal HS each 1/100 second. The stopwatch computes an integer TIME, whose value is the total amount of time (counted in 1/100 second) spent in the "running" state. The program is the following:

```
module BASIC_STOPWATCH :
input START_STOP, HS;
output TIME (integer);
var TIME:=0 : integer in
    loop % stopped state
        emit TIME(TIME);
        await START_STOP;
        do % running state
            every HS do
                TIME := TIME+1;
                emit TIME(TIME);
            end
        upto START_STOP
    end
end.
```

This program computes a local variable TIME, initialized to 0, which will contain the value always conveyed by the signal TIME. This signal is emitted whenever the stopwatch becomes "stopped" (therefore it is emitted at the initialization, so as to give a value to ?TIME). It is also emitted, with incremented value, whenever a 1/100 second occurs in the "running" state. The alternation between the "stopped" and "running" states is realized in a fashion similar to the "flip-flop" program (§2.4.3).

Stopwatch with "reset"

The second version of the stopwatch receives another input signal RESET, whose occurrence puts the stopwatch back in its initial state. ESTEREL allows a modular solution of this problem: whenever RESET occurs, a new basic stopwatch is instanciated. Intuitively, this is like throwing away the old stopwatch and taking a new one!

```
module STOPWATCH_1 :
input START_STOP, HS, RESET;
output TIME (integer);
loop
    run BASIC_STOPWATCH
each RESET.
```

Intermediate time handling

Let us again complexify our example. A new input signal LAP now allows us to record an intermediate time (for instance, the time spent by a runner for one track lap) while continuing to measure the global time. One occurrence of LAP freezes the time on display, while the internal stopwatch time continues to be computed as before. The next occurrence of LAP puts the stopwatch back in a state displaying the running time. Once again, this new version is built from the previous one by putting it in parallel with a "lap-filter." The role of the lap-filter is to manage the display state ("time frozen" or "time running") and to prevent the output of the signal TIME in the "frozen" state. The following program runs in parallel the previous stopwatch — with the signal TIME renamed as INTERNAL_TIME — and the lap-filter, which is again similar to the "flip-flop." Initially, and whenever RESET occurs, it enters the "running time" state, where it transmits any occurrence of the INTERNAL_TIME to the environment. The LAP signal alternatively commutes between this state and the "frozen time" state, where the INTERNAL_TIME is no longer transmitted.

```
module STOPWATCH_2 :
input START_STOP, HS, RESET, LAP;
output TIME (integer);
signal INTERNAL_TIME (integer) in
   run STOPWATCH_1 [signal INTERNAL_TIME / TIME]
|| % lap-filter
   loop
      do
         do % running time
            every INTERNAL_TIME do
               emit TIME(?INTERNAL_TIME)
            end
         upto LAP;
         % frozen time
         emit TIME(?INTERNAL_TIME);
         await LAP
      watching RESET
   end % loop
end.
```

General stopwatch

An actual stopwatch has only two buttons:

- the first one corresponds to the START_STOP signal.

- the interpretation of the second one depends on the global state of
  the stopwatch. When the stopwatch is stopped and the displayed
  time is running, it is interpreted as a RESET command; otherwise
  it corresponds to a LAP signal.

Such a folding of logical inputs onto a small number of physical inputs
is very common in reactive systems. In order to preserve the modularity
of our program, this folding will be entrusted to a "button interpreter,"
which computes the global state of the stopwatch. The corresponding
module is the parallel composition of two flip-flops, computing the "run-
ning/stopped" state and the "running-time/frozen-time" state, with a
process interpreting the signal BUTTON_2 according to these states.

```
module BUTTON_INTERPRETER :
input START_STOP, BUTTON_2;
output RESET, LAP;
signal STOPWATCH_RUNNING, FROZEN_TIME in
    every BUTTON_2 do
        present STOPWATCH_RUNNING then emit LAP
        else % the stopwatch is stopped
            present FROZEN_TIME then emit LAP
            else emit RESET
            end
        end
    end
|| % flip-flop "running/stopped"
    loop % stopped state
        await START_STOP;
        do % running state
            sustain STOPWATCH_RUNNING
        upto START_STOP
    end
|| % flip-flop "running-time/frozen-time"
    loop % running-time state
        await LAP;
        do % frozen-time state
            sustain FROZEN_TIME
        upto LAP
    end
end.
```

The whole stopwatch program is the following:

```
module FULL_STOPWATCH:
input START_STOP, HS, BUTTON_2;
output TIME (integer);
relation START_STOP # HS # BUTTON_2;
signal RESET, LAP in
    run CHRONO_2
||
    run BUTTON_INTERPRETER
end.
```

However, this program is refused by the ESTEREL compiler, which emits the following error message:

```
user error: causality error:
Signals: RESET LAP FROZEN_TIME
```

This signals that our program contains a "causality loop." This type of error is specific to synchronous programs and will be analyzed in the following section.

2.5 Causality problems in Esterel

The synchronous hypothesis may cause temporal paradoxes, similar to short-circuits or oscillations in electronics or to deadlocks in parallel programming. We show here two kinds of such paradoxes, illustrated by short examples.

2.5.1 Lack of behavior

Let us consider the following program:

```
signal S in
   present S then
      nothing
   else
      emit S
   end
end
```

The local signal S must be emitted if and only if it is absent, which is clearly nonsense. This program behaves more or less like a "not" gate with output plugged on input. This kind of phenomenon caused the error in our stopwatch: in the button interpreter, the process interpreting the signal BUTTON_2 decides to emit the LAP signal according to the presence of the signal FROZEN_TIME. Assume that the flip-flop in charge of this signal is in its "do ...upto LAP" statement. Either it emits FROZEN_TIME, and the button interpreter synchronously emits LAP, which should have killed the upto, thus preventing the emission of FROZEN_TIME; or FROZEN_TIME is not emitted, so neither is LAP, and FROZEN_TIME should have been emitted.

The following example of a program without behavior is similar to the positive feedback obtained by plugging the output of an amplifier into its input:

```
signal S(combine integer with PLUS) in
    emit S(0);
    emit S(?S+1)
end
```

The integer value ?S conveyed by S should satisfy ?S = ?S+1!

2.5.2   Multiple behavior

A slight modification of the previous example shows a second kind of
paradox:

```
signal S in
    present S then
        emit S
    else
        nothing
    end
end
```

Now, the local signal S must be present if and only if it is present! There
are obviously two possible behaviors. Below is another program, which
has infinitely many behaviors:

```
signal S(integer) in
    emit S(?S)
end
```

The integer value conveyed by S is completely undetermined. ESTEREL
considers such programs as erroneous, since determinism is one of its
main goals.

   Formally, all these problems come from the fact that the current
event is a fixpoint of some function. Now, since this function is not always monotone, it can have 0, 1, or several fixpoints. ESTEREL semantics (in contrast with most semantics given to STATECHARTS [HPSS86,
HGd88]) only give sense to programs that have one and only one fixpoint. We will see in §5.1 how this feature is statically checked by the
ESTEREL compiler.

2.5.3 Putting right the stopwatch

In order to avoid the causality loop in the stopwatch button interpreter, we only need to admit that the "frozen/running" time state of the stopwatch changes *at the end of the reaction*, when the signal LAP occurs. We have to replace, in the corresponding flip-flop, an interrupt by a withdrawal (cf. definitions, page 18):

```
% flip-flop "running-time/frozen-time"
    loop % running-time state
        await LAP;
        trap T in
            sustain FROZEN_TIME
        ||
            await LAP; exit T
        end
    end
end.
```

Now, when LAP occurs, FROZEN_TIME is emitted before exiting the "trap T" block.

2.6 Another example: the reflex game

2.6.1 Specifications

We consider a machine allowing a player to test his reflexes [Bou91]. The player controls the machine with three commands: putting a coin in a COIN slot to start the game, pressing a READY button to start a reflex measure, and pressing a STOP button to end a measure.

The machine reacts to these commands by operating the following devices: a numerical DISPLAY that shows reflex times, a GO lamp that signals the beginning of a measure, a GAME_OVER lamp that signals the end of a game, a RED lamp that signals that the player has tried to cheat or has abandoned the game, and a BELL that rings when the player hits a wrong button.

When the machine is turned on, the DISPLAY shows 0, the GAME_OVER lamp is on, the GO and RED lamps are off. The player then starts a game by inserting a COIN, which turns off the GAME_OVER lamp. Each game consists of a fixed **NUMBER** of reflex measures. A measure starts when the player presses the **READY** button; then, after a random amount of time, the **GO** lamp turns on and the player must press the **STOP** button as fast as he can. When he does so, the **GO** lamp turns off and the reflex time, measured in milliseconds, is displayed on the numerical **DISPLAY**. A new measure starts when the player presses **READY** again. When the cycle of **NUMBER** measures is completed, the average reflex time is displayed after a pause of **PAUSE_LENGTH** milliseconds and the **GAME_OVER** lamp is turned on.

There are five exception cases. Two of them are simple mistakes and make the **BELL** ring:

- the player presses **STOP** instead of **READY** to start a measure; or

- the player presses **READY** during a measure.

In the other three cases, the **RED** and **GAME_OVER** lamps are turned on, the **GO** lamp is turned off, and the game ends:

- the player does not press the **READY** button within **TIME_LIMIT** milliseconds when he is expected to (one assumes that the player has abandoned the game);

- the player does not press the **STOP** button within **TIME_LIMIT** milliseconds when he is expected to (i.e., after the **GO** lamp turns on; this is also assumed to be an abandon);

- the player presses the **STOP** button after he has pressed the **READY** button but before the machine turns the **GO** lamp on, or *at the same time* that this happens (this is cheating!).

A last anomaly appears if the player inserts a **COIN** during a game. Then a new game is started at once.

2.6.2 Interface

Three parameters of the machine are declared as integer constants: the **NUMBER** of measures and the delays **PAUSE_LENGTH** and **TIME_LIMIT**. They must be defined in the host language. An external function **RANDOM** is

used to determine the random delay at which the GO lamp turns on
after the READY button is hit. The input signals are the millisecond
time unit MS and the three user commands. As far as input relations
are concerned, all input signals are assumed incompatible except MS and
STOP: if the player presses STOP simultaneously with the occurrence of
MS which terminates the random delay, then he must be considered as
a cheater. To control a lamp (say GO), we introduce two output signals
ON and OFF (hence GO_ON and GO_OFF). We also have output signals for
the display and to ring the bell:

```
        module REFLEX_GAME :
        constant NUMBER, PAUSE_LENGTH, TIME_LIMIT : integer;
        function RANDOM() : integer;
        input MS, COIN, READY, STOP;
        relation MS # COIN # READY,
                 COIN # STOP,
                 READY # STOP;
        output   GO_ON, GO_OFF,
                 GAME_OVER_ON, GAME_OVER_OFF,
                 RED_ON, RED_OFF,
                 DISPLAY(integer),
                 RING_BELL;
```

2.6.3   Computation of the average reflex time

We use a submodule to compute the average response time. This simple
module emits AVERAGE_VALUE whenever it receives an UPDATE_AVERAGE
signal with a new measure result:

```
        module AVERAGE :
        input UPDATE_AVERAGE(integer);
        output AVERAGE_VALUE(integer);
        var   MEASURE_NUMBER := 0 ,
              TOTAL_TIME := 0 :  integer in
          every immediate UPDATE_AVERAGE do
              TOTAL_TIME := TOTAL_TIME + ?UPDATE_AVERAGE;
              MEASURE_NUMBER := MEASURE_NUMBER + 1;
              emit AVERAGE_VALUE( TOTAL_TIME/MEASURE_NUMBER)
          end
        end
```

Notice the keyword **immediate**, which ensures that even an update occurring at the initial instant is handled.

2.6.4 The program body

The body is made of two successive parts: some overall initializations and a main loop over a single game that is restarted whenever a coin is inserted. This main loop is simply controlled by an "**every COIN**" statement.

Within a single game, we declare an **ERROR** trap to handle the cheating tentatives and an **END_GAME** trap to handle the normal game termination. Whenever the loop is entered, an instance of the module **AVERAGE** is put in parallel with the main process, with which it communicates by means of the two local signals **UPDATE_AVERAGE** and **AVERAGE_VALUE**. The general structure of the program is thus the following:

```
<overall initializations>
every COIN do
    <game initializations>
    trap END_GAME in
        trap ERROR in
            signal UPDATE_AVERAGE(integer),
                   AVERAGE_VALUE(integer) in
                run AVERAGE
            ||
                <main process>
            end
        end
        <errors handling>
    end
    <end of a game>
end
```

Overall initializations consist in turning off the **GO** and **RED** lamps, turning on the **GAME_OVER** lamp, and initializing the display to 0. The game initializations only differ by turning off the **GAME_OVER** lamp.

The main process of a game consists in performing **NUMBER** measures, and then in displaying the average time:

```
repeat NUMBER times
    <measure>
end;
await PAUSE_TIME MS;
emit DISPLAY(?AVERAGE_VALUE);
exit END_GAME
```

Each measure consists of three steps:

1. Wait for the READY signal within a time limit of TIME_LIMIT. In case of timeout, an error is detected. While waiting, any occurrence of STOP rings the bell (this is the short example given in §2.4.1):

```
% step (1)
do
    do
        every STOP do emit RING_BELL end
    upto READY
watching TIME_LIMIT MS
timeout exit ERROR end
```

2. Wait for a random delay, and after this delay, switch on the GO lamp. While waiting, any hit on the STOP button causes an error. Since an error must be detected even when the STOP button is hit simultaneously with the end of the random delay, the interrupt by STOP is given priority over the random delay. While waiting, any hit on the READY button rings the bell:

```
% step (2)
do
    do
        every READY do emit RING_BELL end
    upto RANDOM() MS;
    emit GO_ON
watching STOP
timeout exit ERROR end;
```

3. Wait for the STOP signal, counting milliseconds, within a TIME_LIMIT delay. In case of timeout, an error is detected. While waiting, any hit on the READY button rings the bell. When the STOP

signal occurs, the GO lamp is turned off and the counted measure is displayed:

```
% step (3)
do
    var TIME := 0 :  integer in
        do
            every MS do TIME := TIME+1 end
        ||
            every READY do emit RING_BELL end
        upto STOP;
        emit DISPLAY(TIME);
        emit UPDATE_AVERAGE(TIME);
        emit GO_OFF
    end
watching TIME_LIMIT MS
timeout exit ERROR end;
```

If an error occurs, the RED lamp is turned on, and the GO lamp is turned off. At the end of a game, the GAME_OVER lamp is turned on. The whole program is given in Figure 2.1.

```
module REFLEX_GAME :
constant NUMBER, PAUSE_LENGTH, TIME_LIMIT : integer;
function RANDOM() :  integer;
input MS, COIN, READY, STOP;
relation MS # COIN # READY, COIN # STOP, READY # STOP;
output   GO_ON, GO_OFF, GAME_OVER_ON, GAME_OVER_OFF,
         RED_ON, RED_OFF, DISPLAY(integer), RING_BELL;
% overall initializations
emit GO_OFF; emit RED_OFF; emit GAME_OVER_ON; emit DISPLAY(0);
every COIN do
   % game initializations
   emit GO_OFF; emit RED_OFF; emit GAME_OVER_OFF; emit DISPLAY(0);
   trap END_GAME in
      trap ERROR in
         signal UPDATE_AVERAGE(integer), AVERAGE_VALUE(integer) in
            run AVERAGE
         || % main process
            repeat NUMBER times
               do % step (1)
                  do every STOP do emit RING_BELL end
                  upto READY
               watching TIME_LIMIT MS timeout exit ERROR end;
               do % step (2)
                  do every READY do emit RING_BELL end
                  upto RANDOM() MS;
                  emit GO_ON
               watching STOP timeout exit ERROR end;
               do % step (3)
                  var TIME := 0 :  integer in
                     do
                        every MS do TIME := TIME+1 end
                     ||
                        every READY do emit RING_BELL end
                     upto STOP;
                     emit DISPLAY(TIME); emit UPDATE_AVERAGE(TIME);
                     emit GO_OFF
                  end
               watching TIME_LIMIT MS timeout exit ERROR end;
            end;
            % normal end :  display of the average time
            await PAUSE_LENGTH MS;
            emit DISPLAY(?AVERAGE_VALUE); exit END_GAME
         end
      end;
      % errors handling
      emit RED_ON; emit GO_OFF
   end;
   % end of a game
   emit GAME_OVER_ON
end.
```

Figure 2.1: The whole program of the reflex game

Chapter 3

Graphic formalisms:
the language Argos

This chapter is devoted to graphical formalisms based on parallel and hierarchic automata. The best known of such formalisms is probably STATECHARTS [Har87], which have been defined by D. Harel and A. Pnueli. However, we prefer to describe another formalism, apparently very close to STATECHARTS: the language ARGOS [Mar89, Mar90], under development at IMAG (Grenoble). This choice is motivated by the following reasons:

- The STATECHARTS semantics seems to still be under discussion [HPSS86, HGd88]. On the other hand, the given semantics is not completely synchronous, since parallel composition may give rise to nondeterministic behaviors.

- ARGOS solves some problems existing in STATECHARTS, in particular those concerning modularity and causality loops. It is a simpler language, whose semantics is completely formalized and thoroughly compatible with the synchronous point of view adopted in ESTEREL.

3.1   Automata and operators

In an ARGOS program, basic processes are finite automata that receive
and emit signals, exactly as in ESTEREL. These automata can be put
in parallel; each of their states can be refined into a process, which is
activated whenever its "father"-automaton enters the considered state,
and which is killed whenever its father leaves this state. In any process,
three kinds of signal are distinguished: *internal signals* are signals that
have been declared local either in the process or in one of its "ancestors";
other signals are either *input signals* of the whole program, in which case
they cannot be emitted by the program, or *output signals* of the whole
program, in which case they cannot be used as input in any transition
of any automaton in the program.

3.1.1   Simple automata

In ARGOS, a simple process is directly described as an automaton
(cf. Figure 3.1). States are named, transitions are labeled, and an automaton has one and only one initial state (signaled by a small incoming
arrow). Transition labels consist of an *input part* and an *output part*,
each of which is made of signals, that belong to a global vocabulary
$E = \{a, b, c, \ldots\}$. The input part is a conjunction of signals (at least
one) and of signal *negations*. The output part can only contain signals.
When the output part of a label is empty, it can be omitted. The intuitive semantics of the automaton of Figure 3.1 is that, when the process

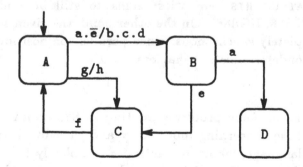

Figure 3.1: An ARGOS automaton

is in state A and if the signal a occurs and the signal e does not, then the process enters state B while simultaneously emitting signals b, c, and d. In this example, {a,e,f,g} is the set of *input signals* of the process, and {b,c,d,h} is the set of its *output signals*. When the process is in state B and if the signal a (respectively, e) occurs, the state D (respectively, C) is entered without any output emission. Clearly, if a and e *simultaneously* occur, the process behavior is nondeterministic. Such an *explicit* nondeterminism is allowed in ARGOS (which only forbids the implicit nondeterminism, involved, for instance, by parallel composition). However, a compiler option enables us to check that this nondeterminism disappears in the whole program (e.g., because a and e are internal signals that are never simultaneously emitted).

3.1.2   Argos operators

Operators on behaviors are tightly connected with design methods. In ARGOS, two design methods are handled by operators: parallel decomposition and hierarchical decomposition.

"Parallel" operator

In ARGOS (as in STATECHARTS), the parallel composition of two processes is noted by drawing them in a box, separated from each other by a dotted line. Figure 3.2 shows two examples, in which involved processes are automata (of course, they could themselves be compound processes).

Process semantics will always be given by means of automata with the same behaviors as the considered process. First, the set of states of a parallel process is the Cartesian product of the sets of states of its component processes. The initial state is the pair of components initial states. Each component runs in an environment made of the global environment and of the other component. In each global state, the global reaction is defined by the following rules:

- Whenever a component can react to an input, it must react. Therefore, the communication mechanism is similar to signal broadcasting in ESTEREL. Depending on the input, either none, or one, or both components participate in the reaction.

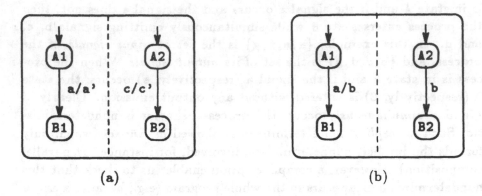

Figure 3.2: Parallel composition

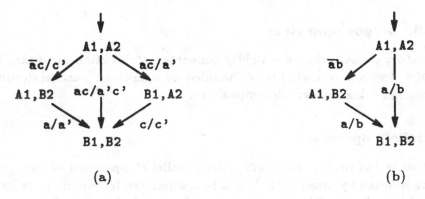

Figure 3.3: Behavior of parallel processes

- When both components react, the global output is the conjunction of components outputs.

- Components communicate with each other during the reaction. Internal signals emitted by each of them are considered as inputs by the other in the same reaction.

Figure 3.3 gives the automata equivalent to the processes given by Figure 3.2, under the assumption that b is an internal signal (since it appears in both the input and output parts of transitions), i.e., a local signal to a "parent" process of the given process.

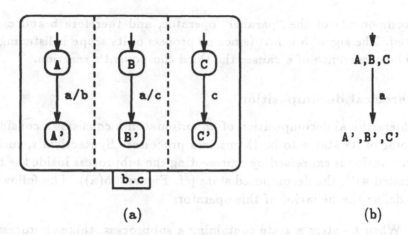

Figure 3.4: Local signal definition

So far, only binary parallel composition has been considered. However, since the parallel composition is commutative and associative, it can be generalized to any number of arguments.

Local signal definition

Some signals can be made *local* to a given process by putting this process into a box (if it is not already in a box) with a cartouche where these signals are indicated (cf. Figure 3.4(a)). This operation has two consequences:

- From a static point of view, these signals become internal to the process and to any of its subprocesses. Therefore, they may appear both in the input parts and in the output parts of their transitions.

- From a dynamic point of view, this operation limits the broadcasting of these signals, which are not transmitted — and cannot come from — outside of the box. This definition is very similar to the local signal declaration in ESTEREL.

Figure 3.4(b) gives the behavior of the process shown in Figure 3.4(a). Since the signals b and c have been made local, a is the only input signal of the process. When a occurs, it causes the reaction of the first two components of the "parallel" operator, and therefore b and c are emitted. The signal b is lost (since no process of its scope is listening to it). The occurrence of c causes the third component's reaction.

Hierarchical decomposition

The hierarchical decomposition of an automaton A consists in considering some of its states to be themselves processes. Syntactically, such a decomposition is expressed by representing the subprocess inside the box associated with the decomposed state (cf. Figure 3.5(a)). The following rules define the behavior of this operator:

1. When A enters a state containing a subprocess, this subprocess is activated in its initial state (it becomes *active*);

2. When A leaves such a state, the subprocess is killed (it becomes *inactive*), and all information about its current state is lost.

3. The signals emitted by active subprocesses of A, if they are not local to these processes, are visible from A;

4. Conversely, any signal visible from A can be seen from an active subprocess, if this subprocess does not have a local signal with the same name; and

5. A subprocess does not participate in the reaction that activates it, but participates in the transition that kills it (the interruption takes place at the end of the reaction).

Let us notice that, from rule 2, the father process can interrupt its subprocesses, whereas from rule 5, a subprocess can commit suicide by forcing its father to interrupt it.

Figure 3.5(b) gives the behavior of the process shown in Figure 3.5(a), under the assumption that b is an internal signal. Initially, the process is in the state X of the subprocess associated with its state A. From this state,

- if signal c occurs and signal b does not, the subprocess enters its Y state while emitting e;

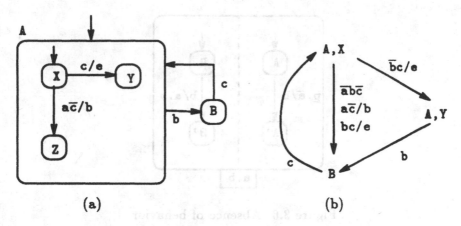

Figure 3.5: Hierarchical decomposition

- if signal b occurs alone, the transition A→B of the father process kills the subprocess (which has nothing to do);

- if signal a occurs and signal c does not, the subprocess enters its Z state while emitting b. This emission of b simultaneously causes the father process to leave its A state (thus killing the subprocess) to enter B; and

- if b and c simultaneously occur, the subprocess performs its transition X→Y while emitting e, and at the same time the transition A→B of the father process kills the subprocess.

When the subprocess is in state Y, the process only reacts to b, which kills the subprocess. Finally, in state B, the subprocess is inactive. It is activated again (in its initial state X) when c occurs.

3.2 Causality problems

As one might expect, temporal paradoxes exist in ARGOS as well as in ESTEREL. Some processes do not have any behavior; other processes present implicit nondeterminism. In the latter case, the detection will

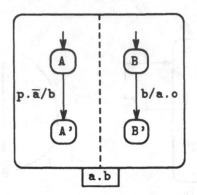

Figure 3.6: Absence of behavior

be a bit more difficult, since the implicit nondeterminism must be distinguished from the explicit one, which is allowed in ARGOS automata.

We only give an example of each type of paradox. A process without behavior is shown in Figure 3.6: if the external signal p occurs when the local signal a does not, the transition A→A' happens, involving the emission of b. Thus the transition B→B' is activated, and a and o are emitted. Now, since a is present, the transition A→A' should not have happened.

Figure 3.7(a) shows an implicitly nondeterministic process: if p occurs, either both transitions A→A' and B→B' are activated, emitting a and b needed for their activation, or neither happens and no signal is emitted (Figure 3.7.(b)).

3.3   Programming style

The hierarchical decomposition mechanism, with interrupt or "suicide," is the only mechanism to kill a process in ARGOS (in contrast with ESTEREL, which has three such mechanisms: simple termination, withdrawal by means of a "trap... exit," and interrupt by means of "do... watching"). The following discussion suggests that this single mechanism can simulate the others; this simulation, however, cannot be

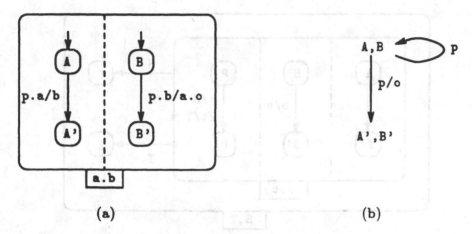

Figure 3.7: Implicit nondeterminism

modularly performed.

3.3.1 Termination by exception

Assume that a subprocess containing states A and A' (respectively, B and B') "abnormally" terminates when signal a occurs in state A (respectively, when signal b occurs in state B). It can signal this abnormal situation by emitting a signal s (respectively, t). Now, an exception handler can be written that kills the subprocess and activates a process managing the exception, possibly taking into account some priority rules among exceptions (e.g., the exception raised by s has priority over the one raised by t). This kind of construction is shown in Figure 3.8.

3.3.2 Normal termination

Normal termination is not built in in ARGOS. It differs from abnormal termination because a "parallel" construct abnormally terminates as soon as one of its components abnormally terminates, whereas it normally terminates only when every component is terminated. In order to express this notion, assume that each component emits a special termination signal when it enters a final state (without successor state).

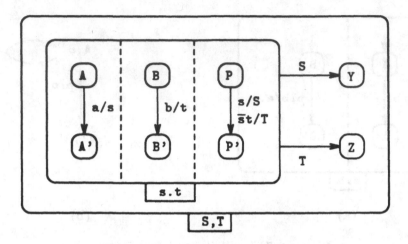

Figure 3.8: Exception handling

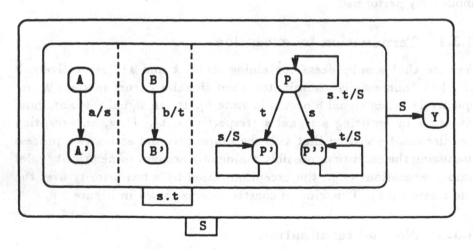

Figure 3.9: Normal termination

Figure 3.9 shows how these signals can be handled to realize the overall normal termination.

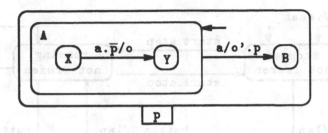

Figure 3.10: Process interrupt

3.3.3 Interrupt

Making a father-process interrupt one of its subprocesses (as performed by a "do... watching" in ESTEREL) is more complicated, since the interrupt must take place *before* the reaction of the subprocess. The proposed solution consists in inhibiting any transition of the subprocess when the interrupt occurs. An interrupt signal (p in the example shown in Figure 3.10) is emitted by each transition interrupting the subprocess, and each transition of the subprocess is conditioned by the absence of this signal.

3.4 Examples

3.4.1 The stopwatch

The stopwatch is not a very illustrative example in ARGOS, on the one hand because it is a single automaton, and on the other hand because the language does not yet allow actions (such as time incrementation and reset) to be placed on transitions. Figure 3.11 only gives the control automaton.

3.4.2 Control logic of the digital watch

A more interesting example, again extracted from the digital watch, concerns the management of the watch running modes [Ber91b]. The watch is driven by means of four buttons: ul, ll, ur, lr ("up-left,"

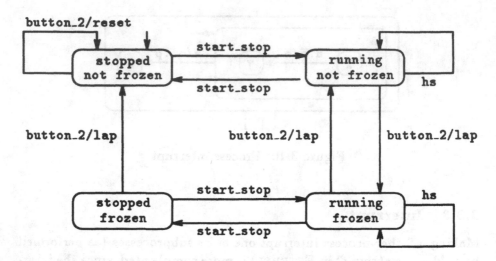

Figure 3.11: The control automaton of the stopwatch

"low-left," "up-right," and "low-right," respectively). It has five running modes, as follows:

- The TIMER mode is the initial one, where the time is displayed. In that mode,

  - the ll button changes to STOPWATCH mode;
  - the ul button changes to TIME_UPDATE mode;
  - the lr button alternatively toggles the time-display mode (24H or AM-PM);
  - the ur button switches the light on.

- In the TIME_UPDATE mode,

  - the ll button changes the updated item (seconds, minutes, hours, etc...);
  - the lr button updates the selected item;
  - the ul button changes back to TIMER mode.

- In the STOPWATCH mode,

    - the ll button changes to ALARM mode;
    - the lr button is the "start_stop button" of the stopwatch;
    - the ur button is the "button_2" of the stopwatch.

- In the ALARM mode,

    - the ll button changes to TIMER mode;
    - the ul button changes to ALARM_UPDATE mode;
    - the lr button alternatively switches the chime on and off;
    - the ur button alternatively switches the alarm on and off.

- In the ALARM_UPDATE mode,

    - the ll button changes the updated item;
    - the ul button changes back to ALARM mode;
    - the lr button updates the selected item.

In any mode, the ur button stops the bell.

Figure 3.12 shows the corresponding ARGOS program.

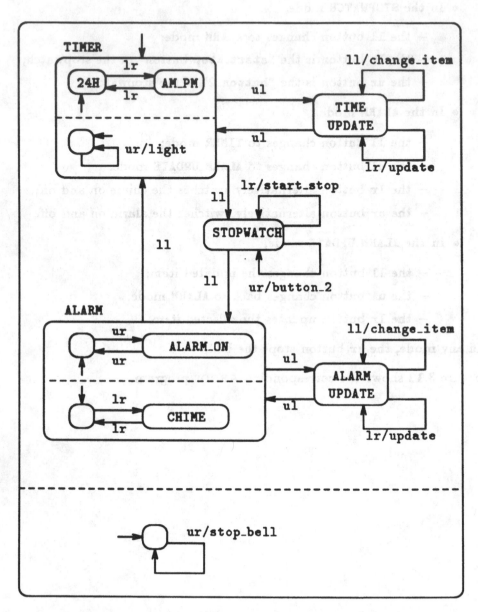

Figure 3.12: The running modes of the digital watch

Chapter 4

Declarative languages : Lustre and Signal

4.1 Introduction

Reactive systems belong to a field in which many users come from control
science or electronics rather than from computer science. It is therefore
appealing to provide these users with description tools that are similar to the traditional tools used in control theory: these traditional
tools often consist, at a higher level, of equational formalisms (differen-
tial or finite-difference equations, Boolean equations, etc...), and at a
lower level, of various graphic formalisms to describe operator networks
(block diagrams, analog schemas, switch or gate diagrams, etc...). All
these formalisms belong to the "data-flow" model, which is well known
in computer science [Kah74, Gra82]. In this model, a system is a network of interconnected operators, running in parallel and activated by
input arrivals (cf. Figure 4.1). This model was initially proposed for
general programming. However, it has not enjoyed much success in this
context, on the one hand because it goes against uses that are firmly
rooted in users'mind, and on the other hand because no reasonably
efficient implementations have been proposed for data-flow languages.
Now, though this model goes against the habits of computer scientists,
it is very natural to control scientists, who must unfortunately translate
their "data-flow" point of view into the classical imperative models used

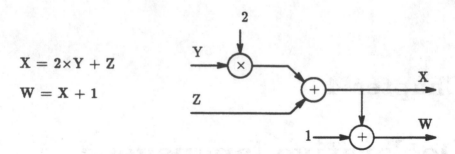

$$X = 2 \times Y + Z$$
$$W = X + 1$$

Figure 4.1: Equational and graphical descriptions of a data-flow system

in computer science. Even from the computer scientist's point of view, the data-flow model has many advantages:

- It is a fine-grained parallel model. Conceptually, as soon as an operator is provided with its inputs, it can compute its output. So the only synchronization constraints come from dependence relations between data. At a time when computer scientists are seeking models and languages that take advantage of the increasing parallelism of computers, it seems paradoxical that some users for whom parallelism is a natural point of view must translate it into more or less sequential formalisms. A fine-grained parallel description allows a wide range of implementations, from the sequential one to the implementation on massively parallel architectures, or even on hardware. It is indeed much more difficult to parallelize a sequential program than to sequentialize a parallel one.

- Generally, data-flow formalisms are "mathematically cleaner" than imperative ones, in which notions such as memory and assignment may involve complex side effects. This mathematical cleanness makes easier the use of formal methods for program analysis, design, and verification.

- An operator net directly provides a graphical representation of programs. Moreover, this representation straightforwardly supports hierarchical decomposition: a subnet can be encapsulated into an operator. The existence of a textual formalism — the equational one — equivalent to the graphical formalism allows the advantages of both approaches to be combined. While the graphical description is convenient at macroscopic levels, it becomes soon extremely complex at detailed levels.

- The importance of hardware implementations has already been outlined. Another advantage of the description using operator nets is that it leads very naturally to such implementations (cf. Chapter 8).

The data-flow approach is consequently appealing in the field of reactive systems. However, most data-flow languages are essentially asynchronous [Kah74, KQ77, Gra82, AW85, Bro89]. A natural way to introduce time in the data-flow model consists in relating the time to the rate of data arrivals. The considered variables can be naturally interpreted as functions of time. For instance, the descriptions given Figure 4.1 express the following relations:

$$\forall t, \quad X(t) = 2Y(t) + Z(t) \quad \text{and} \quad W(t) = X(t) + 1$$

The temporal dimension therefore underlies any description in such a model.

Such a temporal interpretation of data-flow networks involves some semantic restrictions. The maximal reaction time of a program must be measurable, which forbids, for instance, the dynamic creation of processes (which is allowed, e.g., in Kahn's nets). More generally, a synchronous data-flow network should be implementable by means of an *extended finite automaton with bounded memory*. In LUSTRE and SIGNAL, these restrictions result in *clock constraints*.

4.2 The language Lustre

LUSTRE is a textual data-flow language, defined at the IMAG Institute in Grenoble. Its design started in 1984. A graphical programming environment, called SAGA, was developed by Merlin-Gerin Company, which used it to program nuclear-plant control systems. The whole environment SAGA+LUSTRE has been industrialized by the French software company Verilog.

Basic cycles	1	2	3	4	5	6	7	8
Values of C	*true*	*false*	*true*	*true*	*false*	*true*	*false*	*true*
Cycles on C	1		2	3		4		5
Values of C1	*false*			*true*	*false*			*true*		*true*
Cycles on C1				1				2		3

Table 4.1: Boolean flows and clocks

4.2.1 Flows and clocks

In LUSTRE, any variable or expressions refer to a *flow*, which is a pair made of

- a (possibly infinite) sequence of values, of some type; and

- a *clock*, which represents a sequence of instants.

A flow has the nth value of its sequence of values at the nth instant of its clock. Any program (or program fragment) has a cyclic behavior, which defines its *basic clock*, from which any other clock is derived. A flow whose clock is the basic clock takes its nth value at the nth execution cycle of the program. Other, slower clocks can be defined by means of Boolean-valued flows: any Boolean flow can be used to define a clock, which is the sequence of instants where the value of the flow is *true*. For instance, Table 4.1 gives the time-scales defined by a flow C on the basic clock, and by a flow C1, whose clock is the one defined by C. The first row gives the basic cycle numbers, and the second row gives the values of C at each of these cycles. The sequence of cycles on the clock defined by C is numbered on the third row, while the fourth and the fifth rows give the values of C1 on this clock and the sequence of cycles of the clock defined by C1, respectively.

The notion of clock is not necessarily related to physical time. In particular, the basic clock must be considered as defining the finest "grain" of time that the program can distinguish, rather than as a physical time scale. As usual in synchronous programming, the physical time will be perceived as an input to the program: for instance, a Boolean flow, any *true* value of which signals the elapsing of a "millisecond." This point

of view meets the multiform time notion: the millisecond is a flow like
any other, and any Boolean flow can be used to define a time scale.

4.2.2   Variables, equations, expressions, and assertions

LUSTRE variables refer to flows. Each variable is declared with the
type of its values. Any variable that is not an input to the program is
defined by one and only one *equation*. Equations must be understood
in their mathematical sense: the equation "X = E" defines a complete
synonymy between the variable X and the expression E; they have the
same sequences of values and the same clock. This expresses one of
the main principles of the language, *the substitution principle*: such an
equation allows X to be substituted by E anywhere in the program and
conversely. Another basic LUSTRE principle is the *definition principle*:
a variable is thoroughly defined from its declaration and the equation
in the left part of which it appears. In particular, no information can
be inferred from the way the variable is used.[1] A consequence of these
principles is that a LUSTRE program is written as a mathematical system
of equations: the order of the equations is irrelevant, and introducing
auxiliary variables to name subexpressions has no consequences for the
program semantics.

LUSTRE contains only elementary predefined data types — integers,
Boolean, and reals — and a *tuple* constructor. One can use imported
types, defined in a host language and handled as abstract data types,
exactly as in ESTEREL.

Expressions appearing in the right-hand sides of equations are built
of constant, variables, and operators. Constants either belong to predefined types or are imported from the host language. They represent
constant-valued flows on the basic clock.

Standard operators on predefined types (arithmetic, Boolean, conditional operators) are available, together with imported functions. All
these operators, hereafter referred to as *data operators*, can only be applied to operands on the same clock on which they operate pointwise. For
instance, if X and Y are integer-valued flows on the basic clock, with respective sequences of values $(x_1, x_2, \ldots, x_n, \ldots)$ and $(y_1, y_2, \ldots, y_n, \ldots)$,

---

[1] This is the main difference between Lustre and Signal.

the expression "if X>0 then Y+1 else 0" is the flow on the basic clock whose nth value, for any n, is $y_n + 1$ if $x_n > 0$, and 0 otherwise.

In addition to those data operators, LUSTRE has only four *sequence operators* that explicitly operate on flows.

- The "previous" operator "pre" memorizes the value of its argument at the preceding instant of its clock: if $(e_1, e_2, \ldots, e_n, \ldots)$ is the sequence of values of the expression E, pre(E) is a flow on the same clock as E, whose sequence of values is $(nil, e_1, e_2, \ldots, e_{n-1}, \ldots)$, where *nil* is an undefined value (akin to the value of an uninitialized variable in imperative languages).

- The "->" operator (read "followed by") is used to define initial values: if E and F are two expressions on the same clock and of the same type, with respective sequences of values $(e_1, e_2, \ldots, e_n, \ldots)$ and $(f_1, f_2, \ldots, f_n, \ldots)$, "E -> F" is a flow on the same clock as E and F, whose sequence of values is $(e_1, f_2, f_3 \ldots, f_n, \ldots)$. In other words, "E -> F" is initially equal to E, and then forever equal to F.

As a very first example, the equation "N = 0 -> pre(N) + 1" defines the variable N to be initially 0, and then forever to be its preceding value incremented by 1. Since the constants 0 and 1 are on the basic clock, so is N. N is, in some sense, a counter of basic cycles. The following table shows the involved flows:

Basic cycles	1	2	3	4	5	6
0	0	0	0	0	0	0
1	1	1	1	1	1	1
pre(N)	*nil*	0	1	2	3	4
pre(N) + 1	*nil*	1	2	3	4	5
0 -> pre(N) + 1	0	1	2	3	4	5

The last two operators, whose effects are shown in Table 4.2, permit us to define expressions on different clocks:

- The "when" operator is used to "filter" its first argument according to a slower clock: if E is an expression, and if B is a Boolean expression on the same clock as E, "E when B" is a flow on the

	B	false	true	false	true	false	false	true
	X	x_1	x_2	x_3	x_4	x_5	x_6	x_7
Y = X when B			x_2		x_4			x_7
Z = current(Y)		nil	x_2	x_2	x_4	x_4	x_4	x_7

Table 4.2: Filtering and projection

clock defined by B, whose sequence of values is extracted from the sequence of E by selecting only those corresponding to an instant when B is *true*. In other words, it is the sequence of values of E when B is *true*.

- The last operator is used to "project" an expression on a faster clock. Let E be an expression on a clock defined by some Boolean expression B (so E is not on the basic clock). Then "current(E)" is a flow on the same clock as B, whose value at each instant of this clock is the value of E at the last instant where B was *true*. Notice that, for this definition to make sense, any nonbasic clock is syntactically associated with the Boolean expression that defines it.

The body of a LUSTRE program consists of equations and *assertions*. Assertions generalize equations: an assertion is a Boolean LUSTRE expression that is assumed to be always equal to *true* at any instant of its clock. Assertions also generalize ESTEREL relations: they are generally used to specify to the compiler some known properties of the program environment for optimization purposes. For instance, if two input events, represented by two Boolean flows x and y, are known to be exclusive, this can be expressed by the assertion "assert not(x and y)." In the same way, the assertion

```
assert (true -> not(x and pre(x)))
```

expresses that the event x never occurs twice consecutively. Notice the initialization to *true*, which is necessary to avoid a *nil* value: an assertion, a clock, and an output flow may not take the value *nil*.

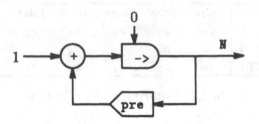

Figure 4.2: Operator net of the counter

Let us remark that an equation "X=E" is equivalent to the assertion "assert(X=E)." Initially introduced for optimization purposes, like ESTEREL relations, LUSTRE assertions play an essential role in program verification (cf. Chapter 9).

4.2.3   Program structure

As mentioned in the introduction, a LUSTRE system of equations can be graphically represented as an operator net. For instance, the equation

    N = 0 -> pre(N) + 1;

corresponds to the net shown in Figure 4.2. This graphical representation naturally suggests a notion of subprogram: a subnet can be encapsulated into a new operator. Such a LUSTRE user-defined operator is called a *node*. A node declaration consists of an interface specification — giving the input and output parameters, with their types and possibly their clocks — and a system of equations and assertions that defines the outputs, and possibly local variables, as functions of inputs.

For instance, the following declaration defines a general counter, parameterized with the initial value, the increment value, and a reset event:

B	true	false	true	false	true
(0,1,false) when B	(0,1,*false*)		(0,1,*false*)		(0,1,*false*)
COUNTER((0,1,false) when B)	0		1		2
COUNTER(0,1,false)	0	1	2	3	4
(COUNTER(0,1,false)) when B	0		2		4

Table 4.3: Nodes and clocks

```
node COUNTER(init_value,incr_value: int; reset: bool)
    returns (N: int);
let
    N = init_value -> if reset then init_value
                      else pre(N) + incr_value;
tel.
```

Once declared, such a node can be used in any expression as a function. One can write

```
even = COUNTER(0, 2, false);
modulo5 = COUNTER(0, 1, pre(modulo5)=4);
```

to define the sequence of even numbers and the cyclic sequence of integers modulo 5 on the basic clock.

A node can return several output parameters; in that case, the result is a tuple. With respect to clocks, in accordance with the data-flow point of view, the basic clock of a node is defined from the clock of its actual input parameters. For instance, the call

```
COUNTER( (0, 1, false) when B )
```

only counts when B is *true*. In that example, the "when" operator is applied to the tuple (0, 1, false).[2] Table 4.3 shows the result of this expression, together with the difference with the expression "COUNTER(0, 1, false) when B," where the node outputs are filtered instead of its inputs.

A node can take input parameters on different clocks. If the clock of

---

[2] An equivalent expression would be "COUNTER(0 when B, 1 when B, false when B)."

an input parameter is not the basic clock of the node, that clock must be a parameter and must appear in the interface. In the following example

```
node N(millisecond:bool;
        (x:int ; y:bool) when millisecond) returns ...
```

the node N takes a Boolean parameter "millisecond" on its basic clock, and two parameters "x" and "y" on the clock defined by "millisecond." A node can also return parameters on different clocks, with the constraint that these clocks must be visible from outside the node.

4.2.4   Causality in LUSTRE

Causality problems, already encountered in ESTEREL and ARGOS, appear in LUSTRE as cyclic definitions: a variable may not instantaneously depend on itself, since the compiler does not give sense to implicit definitions like "X = 3*X + 1." Such a definition is similar to a deadlock. These deadlocks are detected by a single analysis of static dependencies. LUSTRE forbids also "false" deadlocks, such as

```
X = if C then Y else Z;
Y = if C then Z else X;
```

since the exact detection of deadlocks, in the general case, is obviously an undecidable problem.

4.2.5   Some examples

Watchdogs

We will first write three versions of a "watchdog," a device to manage deadlines. The first version receives three events: two commands to switch the watchdog on and off, and a "deadline" event. The watchdog must emit an "alarm" whenever the deadline occurs when the watchdog is on. Initially it is turned off.

All the events are represented by Boolean variables, whose "*true*" value indicates an occurrence of the event. The watchdog is a LUSTRE node, taking as inputs three Boolean parameters "set," "reset," and "deadline," and returning a Boolean variable "alarm." We get the interface:

```
node WATCHDOG1 (set, reset, deadline: bool)
    returns (alarm: bool);
```

Since the equation order is irrelevant, we can first define the output: "alarm" is true when and only when "deadline" is true when the watchdog is on. Let us introduce an auxiliary variable "watchdog_is_on" that records the state of the watchdog. Then we can write

alarm = deadline and watchdog_is_on

The auxiliary variable "watchdog_is_on" remains to be defined. Its initial value is *false*, it becomes *true* whenever the input "set" is *true*, and it is turned to *false* whenever the input "reset" is *true*:

```
watchdog_is_on = false ->   if set then true
                            else if reset then false
                            else pre(watchdog_is_on)
```

Moreover, one can assume that the "set" and "reset" commands never occur at the same time, which is expressed by an assertion. The whole program is the following:

```
node WATCHDOG1 (set, reset, deadline: bool)
    returns (alarm: bool);
var watchdog_is_on: bool;
let
    alarm = deadline and watchdog_is_on;
    watchdog_is_on = false -> if set then true
                              else if reset then false
                              else pre(watchdog_is_on);
    assert not(set and reset);
tel
```

We consider now a second version, in which the watchdog receives the "set" and "reset" commands again, but must emit an alarm when it has remained set for a given delay, counted as a number of basic cycles. The new program makes use of the previous one, providing it with a suitable parameter "deadline": whenever it is switched on, the watchdog initializes a counter to the current value of the delay. The counter is then decremented at each cycle, and the "deadline" is true when the counter reaches zero. It is defined by means of a node "EDGE," of general usage, which returns *true* whenever its parameter has a rising edge (i.e., is switched from *false* to *true*):

```
node EDGE (b:  bool) returns (edge:  bool);
let
    edge = false -> (b and not pre(b));
tel

node WATCHDOG2 (set, reset:  bool; delay:  int)
    returns (alarm:  bool);
var remaining_delay:  int; deadline:  bool;
let
    alarm = WATCHDOG1(set, reset, deadline);
    deadline = EDGE(remaining_delay = 0);
    remaining_delay = if set then delay else
                      (0 -> pre(remaining_delay)-1);
tel
```

Let us finally assume that a watchdog similar to the previous one is desired, but that the delay must be counted according to some time unit, i.e., as a number of occurrences of some event "time_unit." We only have to call WATCHDOG2 on some suitable clock: WATCHDOG2 must perceive any occurrence of "time_unit," any switching command, and the initialization:

```
node WATCHDOG3 (set, reset, time_unit:  bool;
                delay:  int)
    returns (alarm:  bool);
var clock:  bool; let
    alarm = current(WATCHDOG2
                ((set, reset, delay) when clock));
    clock = true -> set or reset or time_unit;
tel
```

From these examples, one could discuss the advantages of such a declarative expression with respect to an imperative one. It is doubtful that an imperative language would allow such a natural and modular expression of this simple problem.

The stopwatch

We will now progressively[3] build the stopwatch program, while attemting to show that the program is straightforwardly derived from its informal specifications.

Simple stopwatch: The first version has only two buttons, "start_stop" and "reset," which will be handled by Boolean variables, as usual. It receives also the 1/100 second by means of a Boolean parameter "hs." It returns a "time" together with its state "running." The program interface is the following:

```
node Simple_Stopwatch (start_stop, reset, hs:  bool)
     returns (time:  int; running:  bool);
```

The computed "time" is initially zero, it is incremented whenever the event "hs" occurs while the stopwatch is "running," and it is reset to zero whenever the event "reset" occurs:

```
time = 0 -> if hs and running then pre(time) + 1
                 else if reset then 0 else pre(time)
```

We could also use the node COUNTER, defined in §4.2.3, called on a suitable clock:

```
time = current(COUNTER((0,1,reset) when clock));
clock = (hs and running) or (true -> reset);
```

The state of the stopwatch is initially "stopped" and changes whenever the button "start_stop" is pushed:

```
running = false -> if start_stop then not pre(running)
                 else pre(running)
```

The whole program is as follows:

---

[3]However, we cannot build the stopwatch with "reset" from a version without "reset," as is done in Esterel. Because of the lack of control structure, the possibility of resetting the stopwatch must be taken into account from the beginning.

```
node Simple_Stopwatch (start_stop, reset, hs:  bool)
   returns (time:  int; running:  bool);
let
   time = 0 -> if hs and running then pre(time) + 1
               else if reset then 0 else pre(time);
   running = false -> if start_stop then
                         not pre(running)
                      else pre(running);
tel
```

General stopwatch: The second version permits us to record an intermediate time. The stopwatch now manages two times: the "internal_time," computed as before, and the "displayed_time," which remains constant when the stopwatch is "frozen" and which equals the "internal_time" otherwise. The "reset" button is used to toggle the state "frozen/not frozen" of the stopwatch. Initially the stopwatch is not frozen; if "reset" occurs when the stopwatch is running and not frozen, it becomes frozen; when "reset" is pushed when the stopwatch is frozen, it becomes not frozen. The "reset" button is interpreted as an actual reset command only when it is pushed when the stopwatch is stopped and not frozen.

The node interface is the following:

```
node Stopwatch(start_stop, reset, hs: bool)
   returns(displayed_time: int; running, frozen: bool);
```

As usual, we start by the definition of outputs. The definition of the variable "frozen" is straightforwardly deduced from the specification:

```
frozen = false ->
            if reset and pre(running) then true
            else if reset and pre(frozen) then false
            else pre(frozen)
```

The "displayed_time" is defined by means of the "internal_time" (a local variable to be defined):

```
displayed_time =   if frozen then pre(displayed_time)
                   else internal_time
```

It can also be defined by using a clock:

```
displayed_time =
        current(internal_time when not frozen)
```

The node "Simple_Stopwatch" is used to define the "internal_time" and the output "running":

```
(internal_time, running) =
        Simple_Stopwatch(start_stop, actual_reset, hs)
```

As stated in the specification, the stopwatch is only reset when the "reset" button is pushed when the stopwatch is stopped and not frozen:

```
actual_reset =
        reset and pre(not running and not frozen)
```

The final program is shown below:

```
node Stopwatch(start_stop, reset, hs: bool)
   returns(displayed_time: int; running, frozen: bool);
var internal_time: int; actual_reset: bool;
let
  frozen = false ->
              if reset and pre(running) then true
              else if reset and pre(frozen) then false
              else pre(frozen);
  displayed_time =
              current(internal_time when not frozen);
  (internal_time, running) =
      Simple_Stopwatch(start_stop, actual_reset, hs);
  actual_reset =
              reset and pre(not running and not frozen);
  tel
```

4.3   The language SIGNAL

SIGNAL was developed in IRISA (Rennes, France) by a team directed by
Albert Benveniste and Paul Le Guernic. SIGNAL has been industrialized
by the Company TNI. Like LUSTRE, SIGNAL is a declarative language,
where a program expresses relationships between timed sequences of
values. However, these two languages differ significantly:

- LUSTRE is a functional language: any program (fragment) — if
  we ignore assertions — and any operator define a function from
  its input sequences to its output sequences. From this point of
  view, LUSTRE is truly a "data-flow" language, since the "input
  flows" completely determine the program behavior.

- In contrast, SIGNAL is a *relational* language: generally speaking,
  a SIGNAL program defines a relation between its input and output
  flows. The way an output flow is used may constrain the input
  flows of the operator that produces it (some operators behave as
  "data pumps"). The programming style in SIGNAL is then close
  to "programming by constraint": any program component induces
  its own constraints, which restrict the nondeterminism of the program. The conjunction of all these constraints must result in a
  deterministic description: this will be checked by the compiler.

Here, we will only give a sketchy description of the language. The interested reader can consult the bibliography [LBBG85, BL90, GGB87,
LGLL91].

4.3.1   Signals, clocks, and operators

A *signal* is a sequence of values associated with a *clock*.

Data domains: In addition to usual scalar types (Boolean, integer,
float), SIGNAL contains arrays of arbitrary dimension with scalar elements, and the predefined type **event**, which has only one value (a
signal of type **event** can only be present or absent; it is similar to a
"pure" signal in ESTEREL).

Clocks: A clock is a discrete set of instants, taken from a totally ordered set. With each signal X is associated a clock C_X, which defines
(like in LUSTRE) the sequence of instants when its values are present.
Therefore, a signal can be viewed as a function from its associated clock
onto its domain of values. $X = (X_t)_{t \in C_X}$.

Given a clock C, let us introduce the following notations:

- $0_C = \min\{t \mid t \in C\}$

- $\forall t \in C,\ t \neq 0_C,\ t \overset{C}{-} 1 = \max\{t' \in C, t' < t\}$.

- More generally

$$t \overset{C}{-} (k+1) = \max\{t' \in C, t' < t \overset{C}{-} k\}, \text{ if } t \overset{C}{-} k \neq 0_C$$

A clock itself can be considered as a signal of type **event**.

Operators: Signals are defined by elementary processes, which are
written using two kinds of operators:

- usual operators (arithmetic, Boolean) extended, as in LUSTRE,
  to operate pointwise on sequences.   One writes "Y := f(X1,
  ...,Xn)." Applying such an operator induces the constraint that
  all of its arguments must have the same clock, which is also the
  clock of the result.

- three specific temporal operators:

  - The delay: "Y := X \$ k" specifies that X and Y have the
    same clock C, and that $\forall t \in C$ such that $t \overset{C}{-} k$ exists, $Y_t = X_{t \overset{C}{-} k}$. Initial values can be specified in the declaration of Y.
  - The extraction: "Y := X when B," where B is a Boolean
    signal, specifies that the clock C_Y of Y is the set of instants
    $t \in C_X \cap C_B$ such that $B_t = true$, and that at each of these
    instants we have $Y_t = X_t$.

— The deterministic merge: "Y := X default Z" specifies that the clock C_Y of Y is the union of the clocks of X and Z, and that

$$\forall t \in C_X \cup C_Z, \quad Y_t = \begin{cases} X_t & \text{if } t \in C_X \\ Z_t & \text{otherwise} \end{cases}$$

An equation is an elementary process. Two operators are used to compose processes:

- The parallel composition: If P and Q are processes, "P | Q" is the process resulting of their parallel composition. This process specifies the conjunction of the constraints specified by P and Q. The parallel composition is commutative and associative.

- The scoping restriction: If P is a process and if X is a signal identifier, "P\X" is the process obtained by considering X as being local to P (i.e., X is not visible from outside P).

Example: The following SIGNAL process builds a signal MIN, emitted each minute, from a clock SEC coming from its environment and supposed to occur each second:

```
(| S := (0 when MIN) default (ZS + 1)
 | ZS := S $ 1
 | MIN := SEC when (ZS=59)
 | synchro {S,SEC} |)
```

Let us explain this example:

- "S:= (0 when MIN) default (ZS +1)": the integer signal S counts the number of occurrences of SEC modulo 60: it is reset to zero at each occurrence of MIN; otherwise it is set to its previous value (ZS) incremented by 1;

- "ZS := S $ 1" defines ZS to always carry the previous value of S; both signals are implicitly synchronous;

- "MIN := SEC when (ZS=59)": the signal MIN occurs whenever SEC happens when the previous value of the counter is 59: MIN occurs every 60 seconds;

- "synchro{S,SEC}" forces the synchrony between the counter S and the input signal SEC: S counts seconds; synchro is an operator without outputs, whose only role is to constrain its inputs to be synchronous.

Remarks:

- The conditional operator is not built in in SIGNAL. Conditional selection can be performed by combining extraction and merge. To express that X equals either Y or Z according to the value of a Boolean signal B, we can write "X := (Y when B) default Z." Notice that this construction is not equivalent to the LUSTRE equation "X = if B then Y else Z," since here there are no constraints on the clocks of Y, Z, and B.

- A specific feature of SIGNAL is the existence of programs that emit outputs at a faster rate than their inputs. In that sense, a SIGNAL program is not necessarily *reactive*: the following process emits 10 occurrences of S for each receptions of E:

```
(| N := (0 when E) default (ZN + 1)
 | ZN := N $ 1
 | synchro{N,S}
 | synchro{E, N when (ZN = 9)} |)
```

4.3.2 Program structure

SIGNAL is a modular language in the same sense as LUSTRE:

- Signals are defined by composing (elementary or compound) processes.

- A set of signal definitions can be encapsulated into a model (like a LUSTRE node) that can be used as a "black box," by means of an interface that describes its static parameters (dimensions, initializations) and its connections (input/output signals).

- Such a model can use other submodels, or even external models that are only known by their interfaces.

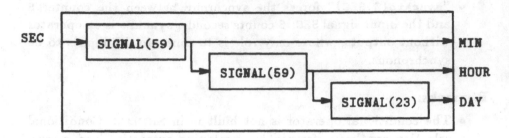

Figure 4.3: Model instanciation

Example: The model SIGNAL contains the process presented above, where the value 59 becomes a static parameter N, and the signals SEC and MIN are renamed into the connection signals IT and OT:

```
processus SIGNAL = {integer N} { ? event IT ! event OT }
(| synchro {S, IT}
 | ZS := S $ 1
 | OT :=IT when (ZS=N)
 | S  := (0 when OT) default (ZS +1) |)
where
   integer S, ZS init N
end
```

To emit signals each minute (MIN), each hour (HOUR), and each day (DAY), one can use this model as in the following process (graphically represented by Figure 4.3):

```
(| MIN  := SIGNAL(59){SEC}
 | HOUR := SIGNAL(59){MIN}
 | DAY  := SIGNAL(23){HOUR} |)
```

Part II

Compilation

Chapter 5

Static verifications

5.1 Causality checking in Esterel

As seen in §2.5, an ESTEREL program can raise some temporal paradoxes, which involve either the absence of any behavior or a non-deterministic behavior. This phenomenon, which appears in all really synchronous languages, comes from the fact that a program reaction, while considered instantaneous, is made up of a sequence of elementary actions (sometimes called "microsteps" [HPSS86]) *that are performed in fixed order*[1]: the first statement of a sequence is performed "before" the second one, a "present S do <stat>" statement checks the presence of S "before" any signal emission involved by "<stat>," and so forth.

In ESTEREL this point of view is expressed by the "execution semantics" [BG88]. Let us sketch here how this semantics allows the detection of causality problems. If we admit that the statements "present," "do ... watching," and any statement containing an expression "?S" correspond to signal readings, while an "emit" is a signal writing, then a signal may only be read, in a reaction, once all the writing of this signal has been performed. In particular, one may not conclude that a signal

---

[1]Another, more formal point of view on these problems is to define the program reaction as the least fixpoint of some function. Microsteps correspond to iterations in the iterative computation of this fixpoint. Now, since the involved functions are not always monotone, it may happen that either they do not have any fixpoint (in which case a "no behavior" paradox appears) or they admit several minimal fixpoints (in which case a "nondeterminism" paradox occurs).

75

is absent as long as its emission by some process remains possible. Answering such a question obviously raises undecidable problems (since a signal emission can depend on conditions involving arbitrary data). The ESTEREL compiler performs an approximate analysis, which can result, in some cases, in rejecting intuitively consistent programs.

This analysis consists in associating with each program fragment a *potential*, which is the set of signals that can be emitted during its first reaction. The definitive status (present/absent) of a signal is only fixed, at a program control point, when this signal does not belong to its associated potential. Actions that read this signal are then freed, and the control advances consequently. When this derivation happens to be blocked because all the processes are waiting for the status or the value of a signal that belongs to the current potential, the compiler detects a causality cycle and rejects the program.

We illustrate this analysis on a program fragment extracted from the Stopwatch, where a causality cycle appears (cf. §2.4.4):

```
        signal FROZEN_TIME in
1           every BUTTON_2 do
2               present STOPWATCH_RUNNING then emit LAP
3               else present FROZEN_TIME then emit LAP
4                   else emit RESET
5                   end
6               end
7           end
8       ||
9           loop
10              await LAP;
11              do
12                  sustain FROZEN_TIME
13              upto LAP
14          end
        end.
```

The first step of the analysis is as follows: Initially, the control is stopped at lines 1 and 10. The corresponding potential is {LAP,RESET,FROZEN_TIME}. Now,

- If the external signals BUTTON_2 and STOPWATCH_RUNNING both occur, when the control reaches lines 2 and 10, the signal LAP is
  emitted. Its status becomes "present," and the second process
  progresses to line 12 and emits FROZEN_TIME (which is ignored
  since nobody listens to it). The reaction terminates with control
  at lines 1 and 12.

- If the external signal BUTTON_2 occurs alone, the control jumps to
  lines 3 and 10 with the same potential. Since FROZEN_TIME belongs
  to that potential, the first process cannot decide its status and is
  blocked. In the same way, for the second process, the emission
  of FROZEN_TIME depends on the presence of LAP, whose status is
  still unknown since it belongs to the potential. Therefore, both
  processes are blocked, and the causality cycle is detected.

5.2 Causality checking in Argos

The ARGOS compiler thoroughly checks program causality. As a matter
of fact, since there are no numerical data in ARGOS, causality checking is
decidable. On the other hand, the problem is simpler than in ESTEREL,
because of some features of the language:

- there is no sequence operator (semicolon);

- there is one interruption operator only; and

- output signals cannot be read.

However, there is a price in complexity: causality checking is quadratic
in ESTEREL, and exponential in ARGOS.

Causality loops are detected when the local signal operator is applied.
Only local signals can involve causality loops, since they can appear in
both the input and output parts of transitions. When some signals are
made local to a process, one must check:

- that the resulting process is *complete*, i.e., that any input event
  (input signal combination) can be accepted in any of its states;
  and

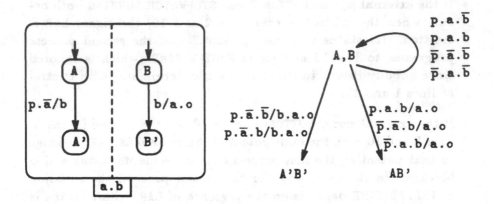

Figure 5.1: Lack of behavior

- that no implicit nondeterminism take place.

Intuitively, the following procedure is applied:

- The whole automaton of the process is built, so that the input parts of the transitions are *complete monomials* of input and local signals.

- Illegal transitions are removed. A transition is illegal in two cases:

  - when it contains both a signal and its negation; or
  - when its input part contains a local signal that does not appear in its output part.

- One checks the existence of one and only one transition from each state and for each monomial of input signals.

Let us illustrate this procedure on the example processes considered in §3.2:

- Figure 5.1 gives the process of Figure 3.6 with its whole automaton. One can easily check that all the transitions involving the signal p are illegal.

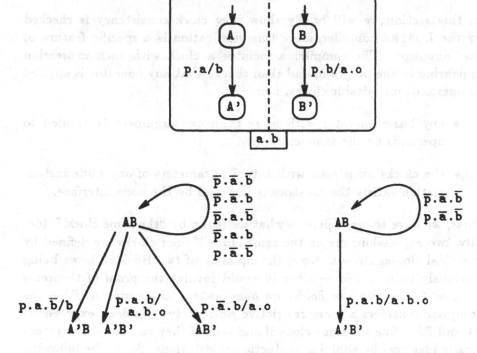

Figure 5.2: Nondeterminism

- Figure 5.2 gives the process of Figure 3.7, its whole automaton, and the result of removing all the illegal transitions. This result is clearly nondeterministic.

This procedure does not distinguish between implicit and explicit nondeterminism. To accept explicit nondeterminism, one can hide it first by introducing some auxiliary signals (whose role is to distinguish transitions with identical input parts), and then apply the procedure, detect the implicit nondeterminism, and remove the auxiliary signals.

5.3   Clock checking in Lustre

In this section we will briefly show how clock consistency is checked
by the LUSTRE compiler, since this verification is a specific feature of
the language. The compiler associates a clock with each expression
appearing in the program, and then checks that any operator is applied
to operands on suitable clocks, i.e.:

- any basic operator with more than one argument is applied to
  operands on the same clock; and

- the clocks associated with actual parameters of any node instanciation satisfy the constraints imposed by the node interface.

First, we have to make precise what we mean by "the same clock." Ide-
ally, two expressions are on the same clock if their clocks are defined by
identical Boolean flows. Now, the equality of two Boolean flows being
obviously undecidable — since it would involve the proof of theorems
such as *"whenever x>y holds, we have z=2*u, and conversely"* — the
compiler considers a more restrictive notion: two Boolean expressions
B1 and B2 define the same clock if and only if they can be made syntactically identical by applying syntactic substitutions. So, in the following
example:

```
x = a when (y>z);
y = b+c;
u = d when (b+c>z);
v = e when (z<y);
```

x and u are on the same clock, which is considered different from the
clock of v.

The rules for computing clocks are formally described in [CPHP87,
Pla88]. These rules satisfy the definition principle: the clock of a variable cannot be inferred from the use of the variable. For instance, the
following program, where M and N are nodes returning results on the
same clock as their inputs contains a clock error:[2]

---

[2]Notice that, if the output of either M or N depends only on the strict past of its
input, this program does not contain a deadlock.

```
        X = M(Y);  Y = N(X);  Z = X+Y+1;
```

As a matter of fact, although one can infer from the definition of Z that X and Y should be on the same clock as 1 (i.e., the basic clock), this information does not result from the definition of X and Y. From their definition, one can only infer that they are on the same clock.

5.4 The clock calculus of Signal

Clocks play a much more important role in SIGNAL than in LUSTRE, since they are used in any conditional definition. In contrast with LUSTRE, where all clocks are built by sampling a faster clock, SIGNAL clocks are implicitly defined by a set of constraints scattered in the program. The goal of the *clock calculus* is the synthesis of these constraints, and the verification of their consistency (they admit a solution) and of their completeness (they admit only one solution). Moreover, the constraints must uniquely determine each clock with respect to a *master clock*, which is not necessarily the fastest one.

Let us first introduce some notations:

- Any signal S has an associated clock, which is noted C_S.

- Any Boolean signal B defines a clock tt_B, which is the set of instants $t \in C_B$ such that $B_t = true$ (so, $tt_B \subseteq C_B$).

Each SIGNAL operator induces clock constraints on its parameters and its result, together with constraints on the values of its Boolean parameters. The following table subsumes these constraints:

1	Y := f(X1,...,Xn)	$C_Y = C_{X1} = \ldots = C_{Xn}$
2	Y := X \$ k	$C_Y = C_X$
3	Y := X when B	$C_Y = C_X \cap tt_B$
4	Y := X default Z	$C_Y = C_X \cup C_Z$

Line 1 expresses that all the arguments of a data operator must be on the same clock, which is also the clock of the result. Line 2 expresses that the \$ operator returns a result that is on the same clock as its input argument. Line (3) specifies that the result of a when operator is present whenever both of its argument are present while the value of its second argument is *true*. Line 4 specifies that the result of a default operator is present whenever one of its arguments is present.

These constraints, together with standard evaluation rules for Boolean expressions, provide a system of equations. In the SIGNAL compiler, these equations are encoded and analyzed in the finite field $\mathbb{Z}/3\mathbb{Z}$ of integers modulo 3, where 0 encodes signal absence, 1 and -1 encode *true* and *false* values respectively , and 1 encodes the presence of a non-Boolean signal. The analysis of such a system of equations provides an answer to some important questions (see [BL90]):

- Does a program admit a behavior? If the only solution of the equation system consists of assigning the empty set to each clock, then surely the program cannot execute. This happens in the following example:

      (| x := a when (a>0)
       | y := a when not(a>0)
       | z := x + y |)

  which provides $tt_{a>0} = C_a \setminus tt_{a>0}$, i.e., since $tt_{a>0} \subseteq C_a$, $C_a = \emptyset$.

- If the program admits a behavior, is this behavior infinite? If some input values are not accepted, the program can deadlock. For instance,

      (| x := a when (a>0)
       | z := x + a |)

  provides $tt_{a>0} = C_a$, which means that the input a must always be positive.

- Is the program deterministic? If there exists more than one master clock, some parts of the program can run at independent rates. In the following example:

      (| x := (x $ 0) + 1
       | y := x when c |)/x

we get only one equation $h_y = h_x \cap tt_c$, which leaves the clocks of x and c unrelated. The variable x is a counter that is not synchronized by any external signal. Thus, its computation rate is left undetermined, and the output y, which samples the values of x when the input c is *true*, can be any subsequence of the sequence of integers.

- If the program is deterministic, is it

  - a function from input signals, where clocks are obtained by sampling a basic clock, as in LUSTRE (this is the case when all the clocks in the solution are functions of the input signal clocks), or

  - a function of input signals that restricts these input signals according to some computed clocks?

A last consequence of the clock calculus is the precise determination of dependencies among variables. The compiler builds a *conditional dependence graph*, which specifies, for any pair (X,Y) of signals, under what condition the signal X instantly depends on Y. The verification that the program does not contain cyclic definition is then made by computing the conjunction of all the conditions associated with each loop of the conditional dependence graph, and by checking that this conjunction is identically false. The detection of causality cycle is then more precise than in LUSTRE, where only static (unconditional) dependencies are considered (cf. §4.2.4).

Chapter 6

Sequential code generation

6.1 The Esterel compiler

The compiling method that synthesizes the sequential code control structure as a finite automaton was first introduced in the ESTEREL compiler. This method was applied later on to LUSTRE and ARGOS. Our presentation basically follows [BCG87].

6.1.1 Principles

The operational semantics of ESTEREL is described in [BG88, Gon88] by means of structural inference rules in the style of [Plo81]. Let us consider an ESTEREL program P containing pure signals only and no variables. If the program does not raise causality problems, then for each input event e, the semantic rules *uniquely* determine the corresponding output event s — which is made of signals emitted by P in response to e — together with a new program Q — which represents the continuation of P after receiving e. The notation "$P \xrightarrow{e}{s} Q$" expresses that "*in presence of the input event e, the program P emits the output event s, and will afterwards behave as Q.*" The language determinism exactly corresponds to the uniqueness of this transition for a given e.

Since P only has a finite and known number of input signals, it also admits a finite number of input events, and any continuation Q admits the same set of input events. Let $\{e_1, e_2, \ldots, e_n\}$ be this set of input

85

events, and let us note $\frac{\partial}{\partial i} P$ the continuation of P (often called *derivative*) according to e_i: For all $i = 1 \ldots n$, we have $P \xrightarrow[s_i]{e_i} \frac{\partial}{\partial i} P$. More generally, for any finite word $w = w_1.w_2 \ldots w_k$ on the alphabet $\{1, 2, \ldots, n\}$, we note $\frac{\partial}{\partial w} P$ the continuation obtained from P after reacting successively to input events $e_{w_1}, e_{w_2}, \ldots, e_{w_k}$. Formally, $\frac{\partial}{\partial w.w_k} P = \frac{\partial}{\partial w_k}(\frac{\partial}{\partial w} P)$. Computing these derivatives simply consists in developing the behavior of P into an infinite tree. The following result states that this tree can be folded into a finite graph:

Proposition 1 *Any program P admits only a finite number of syntactically distinct derivatives, i.e., the set $\{\frac{\partial}{\partial w} P \mid w \in \{1, 2, \ldots, n\}^*\}$ is finite.*

This result is closely related with Brzozowski's theorem [Brz64, BS87] which expresses the termination of the algorithm of the "residual" on regular expressions. The finite graph, whose vertices are derivatives, and whose edges correspond to the relation $\xrightarrow[s]{e}$, is a *finite automaton* whose behavior is equivalent to that of P. Once this graph is built, the derivatives associated with vertices can be withdrawn and replaced by state numbers. In fact, as we will see in the example, each derivative corresponds to a set of control points of the program, and the computation of the next derivatives consists in moving these control points.

For general programs, involving variables and valued signals, the same technique can be applied, but operations on values are considered at a purely symbolic level. Transitions will be labeled by actions on variables and signal values (in fact, transitions are branching, because of conditional statements). A finite control automaton is built, extended with an interpretation that handles the memory operations.

6.1.2 Example

Let us illustrate this method on the "Button Interpreter" of the stopwatch (cf. §2.5.3):

```
module BUTTON_INTERPRETER :
input START_STOP, BUTTON_2;
relation START_STOP # BUTTON_2;
output RESET, LAP;
signal STOPWATCH_RUNNING, FROZEN_TIME in
    every BUTTON_2 do
        present STOPWATCH_RUNNING then emit LAP
        else  present FROZEN_TIME then emit LAP
                else emit RESET
                end
        end
    end
||
    loop
        await START_STOP;
        do sustain STOPWATCH_RUNNING
        upto START_STOP
    end
|| loop
        await LAP;
        trap T in
            sustain FROZEN_TIME
        ||
            await LAP; exit T
        end
    end
end.
```

This program has two input signals, so it can admit four input events,

$$\{\}, \quad \{\text{START\_STOP}\}, \quad \{\text{BUTTON\_2}\}, \quad \{\text{START\_STOP}, \text{BUTTON\_2}\}$$

or, more precisely,

$$\{\text{tick}\}, \{\text{tick}, \text{START\_STOP}\}, \{\text{tick}, \text{BUTTON\_2}\}, \{\text{tick}, \text{START\_STOP}, \text{BUTTON\_2}\}$$

The latter event is forbidden by the relation "START_STOP # BUTTON_2" which states that the input signals are exclusive. The body of the program is first translated into basic statements. The resulting program is shown below:

```
 1   signal STOPWATCH_RUNNING, FROZEN_TIME in
 2      loop
 3         do halt watching BUTTON_2;
 4             present STOPWATCH_RUNNING then emit LAP
 5             else present FROZEN_TIME then emit LAP
 6             else emit RESET
 7             end
 8             end;
 9      end
10 || % flip-flop "running/stopped"
11      loop
12         do halt watching START_STOP;
13         do % running state
14            loop
15               do
16                  emit STOPWATCH_RUNNING; halt
17                  watching tick
18               end;
19            halt
20         watching START_STOP
21      end
22 || % flip-flop "running-time/frozen-time"
23      loop % running-time state
24         do halt watching LAP;
25         trap T in
26            loop
27               do
28                  emit FROZEN_TIME; halt
29                  watching tick
30               end
31            ||
32               do halt watching LAP;
33               exit T
34            end
35      end
36 end.
```

Initially, the control is stopped at halt statements, lines 3, 12, and 24.[1] From this first state (let us call it S_0),

---

[1] In general, this control state is reached after a first step, in which initial values are assigned to variables and which does not properly correspond to a reaction.

- If no input signal occurs, the control does not progress, since no active statement is waiting for tick. So

$$S_0 \xrightarrow{\text{tick}} S_0$$

- If START_STOP occurs, the "do...watching" line 12 is interrupted, and the control of the second process progresses until being stopped by the halt statement, line 16, thus emitting the local signal STOPWATCH_RUNNING, which has no effect. The new global state is made of the halt statements lines 3, 16, and 24. Let S_1 be this state. We have

$$S_0 \xrightarrow{\text{START\_STOP}} S_1$$

- If BUTTON_2 occurs, the "do...watching" line 3 is interrupted. Since neither STOPWATCH_RUNNING nor FROZEN_TIME can be present at that time, the first process emits the output signal RESET, and comes back to the halt statement line 3. So, the global state is again S_0.

$$S_0 \xrightarrow[\text{RESET}]{\text{BUTTON\_2}} S_0$$

Computing in the same way the successor states of S_1, we successively get:

- From S_1, which corresponds to lines 3, 16, and 24,
  - $S_1 \xrightarrow{\text{tick}} S_1$, with a useless emission of the local signal STOPWATCH_RUNNING;
  - $S_1 \xrightarrow{\text{START\_STOP}} S_0$; and
  - $S_1 \xrightarrow[\text{LAP}]{\text{BUTTON\_2}} S_2$, with an internal transmission of FROZEN_TIME, where S_2 is the state where the control is stopped at halt statements lines 3, 16, 28, and 32.

- From S_2, which corresponds to lines 3, 16, 28, and 32,
  - $S_2 \xrightarrow{\text{tick}} S_2$, with useless emissions of STOPWATCH_RUNNING and FROZEN_TIME;

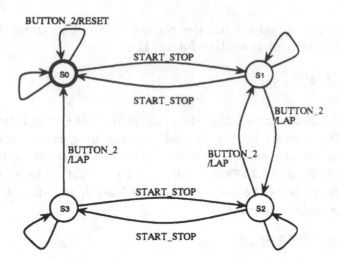

Figure 6.1: The control automaton of the button interpreter

- $S_2 \xrightarrow{\texttt{START\_STOP}} S_3$, with a useless emission of FROZEN_TIME, where S_3 is the state where the control is stopped at **halt** statements lines 3, 12, 28, and 32; and

- $S_2 \xrightarrow[\texttt{LAP}]{\texttt{BUTTON\_2}} S_1$, with an internal transmission of FROZEN_TIME.

- From S_3, which corresponds to lines 3, 12, 28, and 32,

  - $S_3 \xrightarrow{\texttt{tick}} S_3$, with useless emission of FROZEN_TIME;

  - $S_3 \xrightarrow{\texttt{START\_STOP}} S_2$, while STOPWATCH_RUNNING and FROZEN_TIME are uselessly emitted; and

  - $S_3 \xrightarrow[\texttt{LAP}]{\texttt{BUTTON\_2}} S_0$, with an internal transmission of FROZEN_TIME.

All the reached states have been processed. The result is then an automaton with four states, represented in Figure 6.1. The corresponding sequential code could be:

```
      S0:if BUTTON_2 then emit RESET; goto S0
         else if START_STOP then goto S1
         else goto S0

      S1:if BUTTON_2 then emit LAP; goto S2
         else if START_STOP then goto S0
         else goto S1

      S2:if BUTTON_2 then emit LAP; goto S1
         else if START_STOP then goto S3
         else goto S2

      S3:if BUTTON_2 then emit LAP; goto S0
         else if START_STOP then goto S2
         else goto S3
```

6.1.3   Comments

This technique is nothing but an exhaustive exploration of the set of
control states of the program. It can be applied to any language that
forbids the creation of dynamic process (an obvious condition for termination), and thus, to many asynchronous languages. However, in the
asynchronous case, it involves a tremendous explosion of the number of
states, which makes the technique inapplicable in practice. Synchrony
generally reduces this explosion for the following reason: in an asynchronous language, each internal statement corresponds to a transition
leading to a particular state. In contrast, in a synchronous language,
transitions are only triggered by input events, and all the internal statements involved in such a reaction are factorized on the corresponding
transition. All the states that are built are "real" states with respect to
the input/output behavior, and there is no "intermediate" state due to
the internal behavior.

Several remarks can be made about this technique:

- It is useless to minimize the resulting automaton, since experience
  shows that, generally, it is already minimal.

- The algorithm translates the initial parallel program into a strictly equivalent, purely sequential one. Running such a program does not involve any process management, so it is simpler and faster. The whole interprocess communication is compiled away and encoded in the automaton.

- As noted in the introduction (§1.2), automata constitute an ideal execution scheme for most real-time systems. The transition time is near optimal, and does not depend on the size of the automaton. If we know the execution time of the elementary computations put on the transitions, the maximal reaction time can be accurately bounded, and then the validity of the synchrony hypothesis can be checked.

- Many statements, like internal communications, *do not generate any code* in the object program. This is an excellent way to run infinitely fast!

- Once the automaton is built, existing automata-based verification tools [QS82, CES86, BRdSV90] can be applied to it (cf. Chapter 10).

- The correspondence between the source program and the generated code is far from being obvious. The slightest change in the ESTEREL program can involve a complete modification of the automaton. This phenomenon is well known for grammars and regular expressions. It shows that writting automata by hand is difficult and unreasonable.

First implemented in the ESTEREL-V2.2 compiler [Cou90], this technique has been greatly optimized in the V3 compiler, thanks to Georges Gonthier's work [Gon88]. This new compiler uses an intermediate code, called IC [SP90], which is a good candidate to be used for any imperative synchronous languages. A translator of ARGOS into IC has been implemented, that allows the automaton generator to be shared by ESTEREL and ARGOS.

6.2   The Lustre compiler

6.2.1   Node expansion

The LUSTRE compiler generates a purely sequential code. Now, it is well known that, from a concurrent program, sequential code cannot be generated, in general, in a modular way: one cannot sequentialize a concurrent subprogram independently of its context of use. A very simple LUSTRE program (suggested by [Gon85]) illustrates this problem. Let us consider the following node:

```
node two_copies (a,b: int) returns (x,y; int);
let x = a ; y = b end
```

Obviously, there are two possible sequential codes implementing a single reaction of this "program": either " x:=a ; y:=b; "or "y:=b; x:=a;." The problem that arises is that the suitable choice between these two codes may depend on the way the node is called within another node. For instance, for the call

```
(x,y) = two_copies(a,x);
```

which corresponds to Figure 6.2, the first code only is correct.

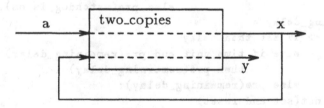

Figure 6.2: A looping call

Thus, before code generation, the compiler first expands recursively each node call in the source program,[2] i.e., replaces each node call by the node body, after a suitable renaming of parameters, local variables, and

---

[2]The Esterel compiler proceeds in the same way, by expanding the "run" statements.

clocks. So, the code generation starts from a "flat" program, without node calls.[3]

6.2.2   Single loop

The most obvious way to translate a LUSTRE program into an imperative code consists in building an infinite loop whose body performs a basic cycle of the program. To obtain this body, one has to choose the variables of the target code (the output variables and the least possible number of local variables, which implement either memories or temporary buffers), to build the actions that update these variables, and to put these actions in the right order, according to the dependencies between variables induced by the network structure of the node. As an illustration of this simple technique, let us consider an expanded version of the program WATCHDOG3 (cf. §4.2.5):

```
node WATCHDOG4(set, reset, time_unit: bool; delay: int)
returns (alarm: bool);
var  watchdog_is_on: bool;  remaining_delay: int;
let
  alarm =  watchdog_is_on and (remaining_delay = 0) and
                pre(remaining_delay)>0;
  watchdog_is_on = false -> if set then true
                                  else if reset then false
                                  else pre(watchdog_is_on);
  remaining_delay =
        0 -> if set then delay
             else if time_unit and pre(remaining_delay)>0
                      then pre(remaining_delay)-1
             else pre(remaining_delay);
  assert not(set and reset)
tel
```

The single loop code could be the following:

---

[3]However, it has been shown in [Ray88] that a Lustre node can be separately compiled thanks to a preliminary restructuring into a set of nodes that cannot be called in loop — and that can thus be separately compiled — together with a main node that subsumes their sequencing constraints. Only this main node must be expanded in the calling program.

```
_init := true;
while true do
  read(set,reset,time_unit,delay);
    if _init then % first cycle %
      watchdog_is_on := false; remaining_delay := 0;
      alarm := false; _init := false;
    else % other cycles %
      if set then
        watchdog_is_on:= true; remaining_delay:= delay;
      else
        if reset then watchdog_is_on:= false endif;
        if time_unit and (_pre_remaining_delay>0) then
          remaining_delay := _pre_remaining_delay-1;
        endif;
      endif
      alarm := watchdog_is_on and (remaining_delay=0) and
               (_pre_remaining_delay>0);
    endif
    write(alarm); _pre_remaining_delay := remaining_delay;
endwhile;
```

Remarks:

- To generate this code, the compiler has introduced some auxiliary variables (whose identifiers begin with an "underscore" character): the variable _init — the value of which is true at the first cycle only, and which is used to implement the "->" operator — and the variable _pre_remaining_delay — which stores the previous value of remaining_delay. Notice that the expression "pre(watchdog_is_on" did not result in the creation of a memory variable, since the compiler found a way to avoid it.

- While it is quite easy to find a computation order that is compatible with dependency relations among variables (the static causality checking ensures that such an order exists), choosing a "good" order is difficult. In particular, the order according to which conditional statements are opened and closed is critical with respect to code length.

- The code speed could be improved. The most obvious inefficiency appears from the fact that the variable _init is checked at each cycle. A solution consists in using more complex control structures than the single-loop structure. This is now discussed.

6.2.3 Compiling Lustre into automata

According to some options, the LUSTRE compiler can improve the code performances by synthesizing a more or less involved control structure. This synthesis is borrowed from the ESTEREL compiling technique, and is based on the following remarks:

- In a declarative language like LUSTRE, control structures, which are available in imperative language, are replaced by operations on Boolean expressions (conditional, clock changes).

- Obviously, if a condition or a clock depends on values of a Boolean variable computed at previous cycles — by means of an expression like pre(B) or current(B) — the code of the current cycle can be made simpler if that value is known. In other words, the code to be executed at the next cycle could be selected according to the current value of B.

The control structure synthesis consists in choosing a set of *state variables*, which are Boolean expressions, and in simulating, at compile time, the behavior of these variables. There are several possible choices of state variables among

- Boolean expressions returned by pre and current operators; and

- auxiliary variables _init_Ck, which represent, for each clock Ck appearing in the program, the expression "(true when Ck) -> (false when Ck)"; these variables, whose value indicates whether the current cycle is the first one on the clock Ck, are used to implement the "->" operators.

Starting from the initial configuration of the state variables, and for each reached configuration, the simulation consists in building a different code for the rest of the program. The result is a finite automaton, whose transitions are associated with the code corresponding to a program reaction. We illustrate the method on the program WATCHDOG4(cf. §6.2.2):

We choose "pre(watchdog_is_on)" and "_init" (an auxiliary variable that stands for "true -> false") as state variables.

1. The first cycle yields "pre(watchdog_is_on)=nil" and "_init=true." Let S_0 be this initial state. Since "_init=true" in this state, all "->" operators evaluate as their first operand. Thus, "watchdog_is_on=false," and "remaining_delay=0." Elementary Boolean computation yields "alarm=false." Furthermore, since watchdog_is_on evaluates to *false*, this will be the value of "pre(watchdog_is_on)" at the next cycle. The next state, S_1, thus corresponds to "pre(watchdog_is_on)=false" and "_init=false." The code corresponding to S_0 looks like:

```
S0 : remaining_delay := 0;
     alarm := false;
     _pre_remaining_delay := remaining_delay;
     goto S1;
```

2. In state S_1, since "pre(watchdog_is_on)" is assumed to be *false*, watchdog_is_on evaluates to *true* if and only if the input set is *true*. Let S_2 be the state where "pre(watchdog_is_on)" is *true* and _init is *false*. The code for S_1 is

```
S1 : if set then
         remaining_delay := delay;
         alarm := (remaining_delay = 0) and
                     (_pre_remaining_delay > 0);
         _pre_remaining_delay := remaining_delay;
         goto S2;
     else
         remaining_delay :=
             if time_unit and _pre_remaining_delay > 0
             then _pre_remaining_delay - 1
             else _pre_remaining_delay;
```

```
            alarm := false;
            _pre_remaining_delay := remaining_delay;
            goto S1;
         endif
```

3. The code of the state S_2, where "pre(watchdog_is_on)" is assumed to be *true* and _init is *false*, is as follows:

```
S2 : if set then
         remaining_delay := delay;
         alarm := (remaining_delay = 0) and
                            (_pre_remaining_delay > 0);
         _pre_remaining_delay := remaining_delay;
         goto S2;
      else
         remaining_delay :=
           if time_unit and _pre_remaining_delay > 0
           then _pre_remaining_delay - 1
           else _pre_remaining_delay;
         if reset then
           alarm := false;
           _pre_remaining_delay := remaining_delay;
           goto S1;
         else
           alarm := (remaining_delay = 0) and
                            (_pre_remaining_delay > 0);
           _pre_remaining_delay := remaining_delay;
           goto S2;
         endif
      endif
```

All the reached states have been processed, so the code generation is terminated. Figure 6.3 displays the resulting automaton.

Remarks:

- The obtained transition codes (particularly for S_0 and S_1) are much simpler than the single-loop code. This reduction is often more impressive for larger programs.

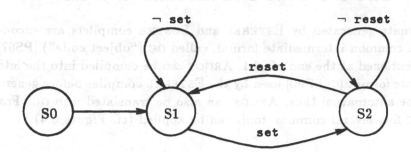

Figure 6.3: The control automaton of the watchdog

- In contrast, the overall length of the code may become very large.
  That is why, in practice, an action code table is built that uniquely
  identifies actions that may belong to several transitions, and transition codes refer to actions by means of their indexes in the table.

- Boolean expressions depending on non-Boolean variables, which
  are needed to compute state variables (integer comparison for instance), are handled as inputs by means of tests on their value.

- Assertions are taken into account. Assertions are computed in
  the same way as state variables, and any branch yielding a false
  assertion is deleted. A state whose total code has been deleted is
  then declared unreachable, and branches already computed that
  lead to that state are recursively deleted. It should be noticed that
  assertions may increase the number of state variables and reachable
  states, as well as increase code length, by involving extra tests and
  computations.

- In contrast with ESTEREL automata, the obtained LUSTRE automata are often far from being minimal. This entails a need
  for minimization. The LUSTRE-V3 compiler uses an original algorithm [BFH+92, HRR91] directly generating a minimal automaton.

6.3   The OC code and associated tools

Automata generated by ESTEREL and LUSTRE compilers are encoded
into a common intermediate format, called OC ("object code") [PS87]).
As mentioned at the end of §6.1, ARGOS can be compiled into the intermediate format IC [SP90] used by the ESTEREL compiler before generating the automaton; thus, ARGOS can also be translated into OC. From
an OC file, several common tools can be applied (cf. Figure 6.4) :

Code generators: Translators to high-level host languages (C, ADA,
...) are available. They generate a procedure whose call performs a
reaction of the automaton. To activate this procedure, one has to write
a main program that handles physical inputs and deals with outputs.
The interface protocol is as follows [BBB89]:

- For each input signal X, the code generator provides a procedure
  I_X, which must be called — with the carried value as parameter
  — to signal the presence of X to the automaton;

- For each output signal Y, one has to write a procedure O_Y —
  taking the carried value as parameter — which is called by the
  automaton when Y is emitted.

The overall structure of the main program is thus the following:

Initializations
Infinite loop
  Input handling
  Call of the selected I_... *procedures*
  Call of the automaton
      (which will call some O_... *procedures by itself)*
end loop

Automaton minimizer: The minimization tool ALDEBARAN [Fer90]
has been connected with the OC code. The resulting tool, called OCMIN,
allows minimal equivalent automata to be obtained in OC, and this is
particularly useful in the case of LUSTRE.

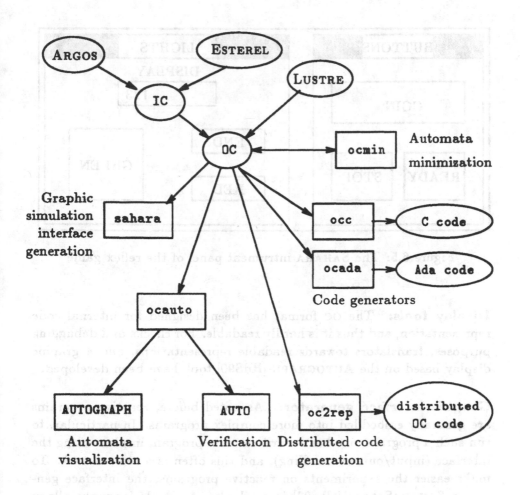

Figure 6.4: The common environment ESTEREL/LUSTRE/ARGOS

Interfaces with verification tools: Automata are a common basic model in many analysis and verification tools for parallel systems. It was therefore appealing to experiment with the use of such tools operating on OC automata. Thus, OC has been interfaced with AUTO [BRdSV90] (see Chapter 10). Some experiments have also been performed with EMC [CES86] and XESAR [RRSV87].

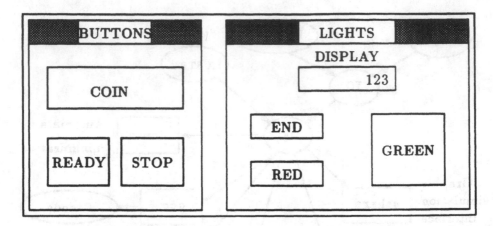

Figure 6.5: The SAHARA intrument panel of the reflex game

Display tools: The OC format has been designed for internal code representation, and thus it is hardly readable. For checks and debugging purposes, translators towards readable representations, and a graphic display based on the AUTOGRAPH [RdS90] tool, have been developed.

Graphic interface generator: As noted before, reactive programs are generally embedded into more complex programs. In particular, to run such a program, one has to write a main program implementing the interface (input/output handling), and this often is a tedious task. To make easier the experiments on reactive programs, the interface generator SAHARASahara [Ghe92] is available. A simple language allows the description of a graphic instrument panel (buttons, lamps, displays, etc.) connected with an OC program. The SAHARA compiler generates a main program that activates the reactive program in connection with this graphic panel. For instance, Fig. 6.5 shows an instrument panel corresponding to the reflex game (cf. §2.6).

Distributed code generation: We will see in §7.3 a method to generate distributed code from an OC program.

Chapter 7

Distributed code generation

7.1 Introduction

Reactive systems are often implemented on distributed architectures, for several reasons:

- the code distribution is imposed by the physical architecture (sensor and actuator localization, protocols, etc.);

- the code is implemented concurrently to improve its performances; and

- the code distribution is performed to achieve fault-tolerance (redundancy, degraded behavior, etc.).

Such a distributed implementation is made of several cooperating programs running on different processors connected by a suitable communication network. Several methods are available to build such programs:

- The separate programming of each processor is a difficult and error-prone task. Settling and debugging a distributed program is difficult, because of the absence of global view on the program state and because of the indeterminism that results from execution and communication times.

103

- General parallel languages, like ADA or OCCAM, allow an easy programming of distributed systems, since no assumption is made on the target architecture. A program can be developed and debugged on a single processor, and then implemented on a network of communicating processors. However, to achieve this transparency with respect to the actual architecture, these languages are nondeterministic, which makes program development more difficult.

The automatic distribution of a synchronous, deterministic program is difficult. We briefly describe two very different approaches, which have been initially proposed, respectively, for SIGNAL and LUSTRE.

7.2   Code distribution in Signal

The code distribution proposed for SIGNAL is based on the structure of the source program. Ideally, from a program P = (|P1|P2|...|Pn|), we would like to obtain a sequential code for each process Pi, in such a way that the parallel execution of these codes implements the initial program. However, such a translation is not possible, in general, for the same reasons that make impossible the separate compilation (cf. §6.2.1): Let us consider, for instance, the following program:

```
P = (| y := g(b) | x := f(a) |)
```

where f and g are arbitrary functions. As in the example considered in §6.2.1, two sequential codes are possible:

```
loop
    read(b); y:= g(b); write(y);
    read(a); x:= f(a); write(x)
end
```

and

```
loop
    read(a); x:= f(a); write(x)
    read(b); y:= g(b); write(y);
end
```

but if P is executed in parallel with the program Q = (| a := h(y) |), the latest code will involve a deadlock, since P waits for a value for a, while Q needs y to compute a. However, let us notice that the program

$$P|Q = (|\ a := h(y)\ |\ y := g(b)\ |\ x := f(a)\ |)$$

may be restructured into (| R | S |), where

$$R = (|\ a := h(y)\ |\ y := g(b)\ |)$$

and

$$S = (|\ x := f(a)\ |)$$

For this structure, one can separately generate sequential codes for R and S, without regards to their running context. As a matter of fact, these processes have the property that all their outputs instantly depend on all their inputs. No running context can introduce an instantaneous dependence from an output to an input, without involving an intrinsic deadlock in the global program.

This simple example illustrates the problem we are faced with. We want to restructure a program into a set of parallel processes, each of which having the following property. Let "$\succ$" be the partial order expressing the instantaneous dependence between inputs and outputs of a process: "$i \succ o$" (or $\{i, o\} \in$ "$\succ$") means that the current value of the input i is needed in the current computation of the output o. We want "$\succ$" to be strengthened into a total order $>$, in such a way that, for any pair $\{o, i\}$, if the relation "$>$" augmented with the pair $\{o, i\}$ is no longer an order, neither is "$\succ$" augmented with $\{o, i\}$. In other words, the desired property states that there exists a sequential code such that any legal (deadlock-free) loop from an output into an input does not induce a deadlock in the sequential code.

7.2.1   Static dependences

First, we only consider static dependences (without clocks). This case has been studied in [Ray88] to separately compile LUSTRE programs. Two solutions can be applied:

Functional restructuring: A process is said to be "functional" if all its outputs instantly depend on all its inputs. Such a process can only be started, at a given cycle, when all its input values are available (no legal loop). The sequential code corresponding to an execution cycle can be generated as a function, taking all the input values as parameters and returning all the output values.

In our example, the processes R and S are functional. The corresponding functions are

$$F_R = \text{read(b); y := g(b); a := h(y); write(y); write(a)}$$
$$F_S = \text{read(a); x := f(a); write(x)}$$

Coroutine restructuring: Let o be an output of the process. Let $I(o)$ be the set of inputs needed for computing the current value of o ($I(o) = \{i \mid i \succ o\}$). We define the following partial order among the process outputs:

$$o \gg o' \quad \Longleftrightarrow \quad I(o) \supseteq I(o')$$

Then, if $o \gg o'$, any loop of o onto an input belonging to $I(o')$ is illegal, since it introduces a deadlock on o. So o can be computed after o' without introducing additional deadlocks. This remark entails the following result: if the relation "$\gg$" is a total order, the process can be translated into a coroutine — reading its inputs and emitting its outputs within its execution cycle. The code is generated by dealing with outputs according to increasing "$\gg$" order; dealing with an output o consists in generating the code that reads the inputs that are strictly needed to compute o and still unavailable, together with the code that computes and emits o. For instance, let us consider the process

$$P' = (\mid y := g(b) \mid x := f(a,b) \mid)$$

We have

$$I(y) = \{b\} \subseteq \{a,b\} = I(x)$$

so, $x \gg y$. The coroutine code for P' could be

```
read(b); y := g(b); write(y);
read(a); x := f(a,b); write(x)
```

which allows an external loop from y onto a.

7.2.2 Dynamic dependences

The solution actually applied in SIGNAL is more complicated, since it does not only consider static dependences. Dependence relations among variables are now conditioned by clocks (cf. §5.4). Let us note "$X \succ_h Y$" the fact that at any instant of the clock h, the value of Y depends of the current value of X. This relation is extended to any pair (i, o) of input/output variables: A *dependence path* from i to o is any set of variables $c = \{X0, X1, \ldots, Xk\}$ such that

$$i = X0 \succ_{h_1} X1 \succ_{h_2} \ldots \succ_{h_k} Xk = o$$

Let

$$h(c) = \bigcap_{1 \leq i \leq k} h_i$$

and let $C(i, o)$ be the set of dependence pathes from i to o. Then the input/output conditional dependence relation is defined by

$$i \succ_h o \quad \text{iff} \quad h = \bigcup_{c \in C(i,o)} h(c) \neq \emptyset$$

An analysis of these input/output conditional dependence relations provides a partition of the set of instants, and, when possible, allows the generation of a coroutine code, whose sequential ordering varies according to clock values. The SIGNAL distributed code generator restructures a program into processes that can be compiled into such coroutines and that are activated by a control process. The physical distribution is then performed by the tool SYNDEX [GMP$^+$90], which provides also a measure of the performances of the distributed code. Further details can be found in [LGLL91, LeG89].

7.3 OC code distribution

We consider now another approach to generate distributed code, which was initially developed for LUSTRE [BCP88]. In fact, it works on the

common object code OC (cf. §6.3), and so it can also be applied to
ESTEREL and ARGOS.

This approach aims at generating a distributed code when the distribution is imposed a priori. Thus, we do not look for a "good" distribution with respect to performance improvement. We assume that
a set $\{s_1, \ldots, s_n\}$ of execution sites (processors) is given, and that the
user (or an optimization tool) has associated an execution site with each
action of the OC automaton. For LUSTRE programs, this association is
specified by assigning a computation site to each variable of the main
node. Propagating this assignment inside internal nodes provides a site
assignment for each variable in the expanded program.[1]

In the remainder of this section, we will assume that each site is
responsible for the computation of some variables.

The basic idea of the method is extremely simple:

- the code of the automaton is replicated on each site;

- on each replication, the instructions that do not concern the considered site are erased;

- for any pair (s_i, s_j) of sites, since we know in what order s_i computes its own variables and in what order s_j uses these variables,
  we can introduce statements to communicate values computed by
  s_i and used by s_j, without introducing deadlocks. These communications are made by simple FIFO queues; and

- auxiliary "dummy" communications are added for synchronization.

The communication scheme consists of a queue for each ordered pair of
sites. The processor of the site s_i can send a value **v** to the site s_j by
executing a statement "put(**v**,j)"; this corresponds to writing **v** in the
$Q_{i,j}$ queue, and does not involve any waiting. s_j can read and extract
the first value in the $Q_{i,j}$ queue by performing "get(i)"; if the queue is
empty, this statement stops the processor until s_i writes a value on the
queue.

---

[1]The syntactic means to specify a site assignment in Esterel and Argos remain to
be studied.

Using a short example, let us sketch the method to generate the code. We consider a transition of an OC automaton,[2] and we show how this code is distributed on three sites. We give the transition code, with the index of the concerned sites in front of each statement (control statements concern all the sites):

```
read(I1);            (1)
read(I2);            (2)
read(I3);            (3)
L3 := F(I2);         (3)
O2 := G(I2,L3);      (2)
if I3 then           (1,2,3)
    O3 := true;      (3)
    O1 := H(I1,L3);  (1)
    goto STATE2;     (1,2,3)
else
    O3 := K(I1,I2);  (3)
    goto STATE1;     (1,2,3)
```

7.3.1 Code replication

The code is copied in three versions (one for each site). In each copy, we erase the statements that do not concern the considered site; however, when the erased statement uses some variables that are computed on that site, this information is recorded (as a comment). The result is shown in Table 7.1.

7.3.2 Placement of emission statements

First, we place, in each copy, the emission statements ("put"). We use the information about the variables computed by the considered site and used by the other sites. The following strategy is used: Values are emitted as soon as possible (in order to minimize the possible waiting) but only when needed. The informations concerning variable uses are propagated backward in the program: when a variable is computed by the current statement, if it appears in the list of variables used by some

---

[2] Of course, we use a readable version of the OC code.

Code of s_1	Code of s_2	Code of s_3
`read(I1);`		
	`read(I2);`	
		`read(I3);`
	`% 3 uses I2 %`	`L3 := F(I2);`
	`02 := G(I2,L3);`	`% 2 uses L3 %`
		`% 1 and 2 use I3 %`
`if I3 then`	`if I3 then`	`if I3 then`
		`    03 := true;`
`    01 := H(I1,L3);`		`% 1 uses L3 %`
`    goto STATE2;`	`    goto STATE2;`	`    goto STATE2;`
`else`	`else`	`else`
`% 3 uses I1 %`	`% 3 uses I2 %`	`    03 := K(I1,I2);`
`    goto STATE1;`	`    goto STATE1;`	`    goto STATE1`

Table 7.1: Code replication

other sites, it is sent to them and removed from the lists; the remainder of the lists is back-propagated to the previous statement. If the statement is a conditional, we get two lists L_{then} and L_{else} of used variables, corresponding to the two branches of the conditional. In the "then" (respectively, "else") branch, the variables belonging to $L_{then} \setminus L_{else}$ (respectively, $L_{else} \setminus L_{then}$) are emitted, and the intersection $L_{then} \cap L_{else}$ is back-propagated. We give in Table 7.2 the result on our example.

7.3.3 Useless emission elimination

The preceding procedure sometimes causes useless value emission. In our example, it is the case of the second emission of I2 from s_2 to s_3. It is due to the fact that s_3 uses I2 twice, the second use being conditional. Thus, we can withdraw any emission of a variable that is already known by the receiver site, as long as this variable has not been updated since its last emission. This elimination process uses a forward propagation of the available variables of each site: At the beginning of the transition, the sites do not know any variable value. After a "put(X, j)" statement, the site s_j knows the value of X but loses it after each assignment to X. Any "put(X, j)" statement executed when s_j knows X can be withdrawn.

Code of s_1	Code of s_2	Code of s_3
read(I1);		
	read(I2);	
	put(I2,3);	read(I3);
		put(I3,1);
		put(I3,2);
		L3 := F(I2);
	02 := G(I2,L3);	put(L3,2);
if I3 then	if I3 then	if I3 then
		put(L3,1);
		03 := true;
01 := H(I1,L3);		
goto STATE2;	goto STATE2;	goto STATE2;
else	else	else
put(I1,3);	put(I2,3);	03 := K(I1,I2);
goto STATE1;	goto STATE1;	goto STATE1

Table 7.2: Placement of emission statements

This procedure eliminates the last "put(I2,3)" in the code of s_2.

7.3.4 Placement of receiving statements

We have now to insert the "get" statements, so that, on each site s_i, the statements "x = get(j)" appear in the same order as the statements "put(x,i)" in the code of s_j. If the communication network is assumed to preserve the message order, then the transmitted value will always correspond to the same variable on both sites, without need of any additional identification.

The algorithm for placing the "get" statements is the following: We simulate the state of each queue $Q_{i,j}$, i.e., the list of variables emitted from s_i to s_j and still unread by s_j. These images of the queues are propagated forward in the global program as follows:

- Each "put(x,j)" statement performed by s_i adds the identifier x at the end of (the image of) $Q_{i,j}$.

- When s_j has to perform a statement using a variable x that belongs to s_i, then one of the three following situations occurs:

1. The identifier x does not appear in $Q_{i,j}$. Since its value has necessarily been emitted, therefore the value has already been read (by a "x = get(i)" statement), and there is nothing to do.

2. x appears in front of $Q_{i,j}$, and a "x = get(i)" must be inserted to extract the value. The identifier is removed from the (image of) the queue.

3. Other identifiers appear before x in $Q_{i,j}$. The corresponding values must be extracted first, by means of a sequence of "get" statements.

- When a conditional is opened, the queue images are duplicated along each branch.

- Before closing a conditional, the suitable "get" statements are inserted on each branch, so that the queue images become the same. The complements of the greatest common suffix are extracted.

This algorithm is illustrated in Table 7.3.

7.3.5   Synchronization

The method applied so far provides a deadlock-free distributed program, whose functional semantics is the same as the initial program. However, nothing ensures that the temporal semantics is preserved. For instance, if some sites produce value to other sites only, they can take an arbitrary lead over other sites ("pipeline" behavior). The notion of cycle of the initial program is lost, and such a behavior may need unbounded communication queues. Several synchronization solutions can be proposed, according to the degree of "time fidelity" we want to achieve, with respect to the centralized program:

Strict synchronization: To strictly preserve the temporal semantics of the initial program, no process may start its $(n+1)$th reaction before all the others have terminated their nth reaction. To ensure this property, we have to force synchronization, for instance by introducing some

Code of s_1	Code of s_2	Code of s_3	Q_{12}	Q_{13}	Q_{21}	Q_{23}	Q_{31}	Q_{32}
read(I1);	read(I2);	read(I3);					I3	I3
	put(I2,3);	put(I3,1);				I2	I3	I3
		put(I3,2);				I2	I3	I3
		I2:=get(2);				I2	I3	L3,I3
		L3:=F(I2);					I3	I3
		put(L3,2);	I1				L3	L3
I3:=get(3);	I3:=get(3);							
if I3 then	L3:=get(3);	if I3 then						
	O2:=G(I2,L3);	put(L3,1);						
L3:=get(3);	if I3 then	O3:=true;						
O1:=H(I1,L3);								
goto STATE2;	goto STATE2;	goto STATE2;						
else	else	else						
put(I1,3);	goto STATE1;	goto STATE1;		I1				
goto STATE1;		I1:=get(1);						
		O3:=K(I1,I2);						
		goto STATE1						

Table 7.3: Placement of receiving statements

additional "dummy" communications at the beginning of the reaction, so that any ordered pair of processes are connected by the transitive closure of the relation "s_i *has emitted a dummy message to s_j.*"

Weak synchronization: To avoid the proliferation of dummy messages needed in the preceding case, one can prefer a weaker property: the nth reactions of two arbitrary processes must overlap. If the problem specifications can tolerate such a loose temporal interpretation, the corresponding synchronization is much less expensive, because the normal communications participate in the synchronization: if a value is transmitted from s_i to s_j, then the emission precedes the reception. An analysis of these precedence relations allows the determination of a reduced set of additional "dummy" communications that ensures the weak synchronization. In our example, the solution given in Table 7.4 only adds two dummy communications — one from s_1 to s_2 and one from s_2 to s_1 — to ensure the weak synchronization, since

- the beginning of the reaction of s_1 precedes the emission of the dummy message by s_1, which precedes the reception of the dummy message by s_2, which precedes both

  - the end of the reaction of s_2, and
  - the emission of I2 from s_2 to s_3, which precedes the reception of I2 by s_3, which precedes the end of the reaction of s_3;

- the beginning of the reaction of s_2 precedes the dummy communication between s_2 and s_1 which precedes the end of the reaction of s_1; and

- s_2 and s_3 exchange messages.

7.3.6 Final processing

Applying this method to each transition of the initial OC automaton, we get n communicating OC programs, whose cooperation exactly implements the semantics of the initial program. Each program can separately be optimized (for instance, by minimizing the corresponding automaton) without modifying the global behavior.

Code of s_1	Code of s_2	Code of s_3
`put_dummy(2);` `read(I1);`	`put_dummy(1);`	

	`read(I2);`
	`get_dummy(1);`
	`put(I2,3);`
		`read(I3);`
		`put(I3,1);`
		`put(I3,2);`
		`I2 := get(2);`
		`L3 := F(I2);`
		`put(L3,2);`

	`I3 := get(3);` `L3 := get(3);`	
`I3 := get(3);` `if I3 then`	`02 := G(I2,L3);` `if I3 then`	`if I3 then` `put(L3,1);`

`L3 := get(3);`
`01 := H(I1,L3);`
`get_dummy(2);`
`goto STATE2;`
	`goto STATE2;`	`03 := true;`
		
		`goto STATE2;`

`else` `put(I1,3);`	`else`	`else`

`get_dummy(2);`
`goto STATE1;`
	`goto STATE1;`	`I1 := get(1);`
		`03 := K(I1,I2);`
		`goto STATE1`

Table 7.4: Example of distributed code

Chapter 8

Circuit generation from synchronous programs

8.1   Introduction

As noted in the first chapter, the problem of time constraints in synchronous programming reduces to the property that the maximum reaction time of a program is shorter than the minimum delay separating two successive external events. Minimizing this reaction time is therefore a basic goal in compiling a synchronous program. The compilation into extended automata is a software approach to that goal. Another, more radical approach to obtain very short reaction times consists in implementing a synchronous program on a circuit. Synchronous languages are good candidates for silicon compiling, since most circuits can be considered as synchronous machines from some level of abstraction. Some synchronous languages [BC85, BL85] have been designed to describe hardware.

One can wonder about the practical value of a hardware implementation because of the cost of circuit manufacturing. A first answer to this question has already been given : in practice, many reactive systems are actually implemented, at least in part, on hardware. Another answer is provided by new *configurable circuits* ("field programmable gate arrays)." The hardware implementations of ESTEREL and LUSTRE, which are described in this chapter, are tested on a *Programmable Active*

117

Memory (PAM [BRV90]) designed in the Paris Research Laboratory of Digital Equipment Corp. (DEC-PRL). The PAM is a board that can be configured into any circuit by loading a bit-stream — an operation that requires only a few milliseconds. The reaction times of the resulting circuit are then of the order of 50-200 nanoseconds.

An implementation of LUSTRE on the PAM [RH91a] will be presented first, since it is very simple thanks to the data-flow nature of the language. Then we will present the hardware implementation of ESTEREL [Ber91a], which can be viewed as a translation of ESTEREL into LUSTRE.

8.2   Implementing Lustre on a programmable active memory

8.2.1   Programmable active memories

The general concept of "programmable active memory" is defined as follows in [BRV90]:

> A PAM is a uniform matrix of identical cells, all connected in the same repetitive fashion. Each cell, called a PAB (for "programmable active bit)," must be general enough so that the following holds true: Any synchronous digital circuit can be realized (through suitable programming) on a large enough PAM for a slow enough clock.

To support intuition, we will consider a particular PAM, each PAB of which has (see Figure 8.1(a)):

- Four bits of input $< i_0, i_1, i_2, i_3 >$

- One bit of output O

- A one-bit register (flip-flop) with input R and output r, synchronized on the PAM 's global clock

- A universal combinatorial gate, with inputs $< i_0, i_1, i_2, i_3, r >$ and outputs $< O, R >$. This gate can be configured into any Boolean function with five inputs and two outputs, by means of $2 \times 2^5 = 64$ control bits, which specify the truth table of the function.

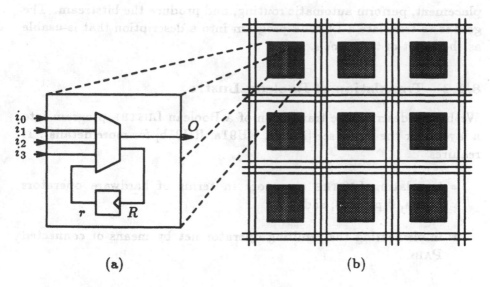

$$i_0$$
$$i_1$$
$$i_2$$
$$i_3$$

(a)   (b)

Figure 8.1: A simple programmable active memory

Between the rows and the columns of cells, there are communication lines (see Figure 8.1(b)) to which the pins of the cells can be connected. These connections and the connections between horizontal and vertical lines can also be configured by means of additional control bits.

Such a PAM, with n active bits, can be configured by downloading a sequence of control bits to configure the PABs and their connections.

We will keep this simple model as intuitive support, although the actual target machine of the prototype compilers is slightly more complicated. The target machine is the *Perle* family, studied and built in DEC-PRL, and based on Logic Cell Arrays designed by Xilinx Inc. [Xil88]. The presently available *Perle-0* prototype is a matrix of 40×80 (double) PABs, and the next version will be about four times larger.

Building the control bitstream corresponding to a given circuit configuration is, of course, a nontrivial problem, in spite of available tools. In the case of *Perle*, the standard tools provided by Xilinx, together with the tools developed in DEC-PRL, take as input a logical description of each PAB, together with optional placement indications. They finish the placement, perform automatic routing, and produce the bitstream. The goal is to translate a LUSTRE program into a description that is usable as the input of these tools.

8.2.2   Translation of Boolean Lustre

We briefly describe the translation of a Boolean LUSTRE program into a layout for the PAM (see [Roc89, RH91a, RH91b] for more details). It requires

- translating LUSTRE operators in terms of hardware operators (gates, flip-flops); and

- implementing the resulting operator net by means of connected PABs.

Translation of Lustre operators

The first step of the compilation of a Boolean program consists in translating its corresponding operator net into a net of gates and flip-flops.

The operator net corresponding to a Boolean LUSTRE program contains Boolean operators (or, and, not, =), conditional (if_then_else), and temporal (pre, ->) operators.[1]

Notice that what we call "Boolean operators" in LUSTRE are not strictly Boolean because of the undefined value *nil*. However, although most of the LUSTRE operators are strict with respect to *nil*, in a legal LUSTRE program, the occurrence of a *nil* value may not influence the outputs of the program. This property is checked by the compiler. So, in a legal program we can replace the undefined value by any Boolean value without changing the outputs of the program. As a consequence, LUSTRE Boolean operators can be straightforwardly translated into gates. The conditional operator can also be translated into a set of gates, using the Boolean identity

        if A then B else C = (B and A) or (C and not A)

---

[1]We do not consider clocks here, though they are not much more difficult to implement.

The "previous" operator will be obviously implemented by means of a flip-flop (noted "Flop"). In the technology used, the initial value of flip-flops is 0, so *nil* is considered to be 0. The "followed-by" operator is implemented by means of the *reset* input of the circuit:

```
A -> B = if RESET then A else B
       = (RESET and A) or (not RESET and B)
```

For instance, the equation

```
watchdog_is_on = false -> if set then true
                          else if reset then false
                          else pre(watchdog_is_on)
```

will be translated into

```
watchdog_is_on =
    (false and RESET) or
        (not RESET and ((true and set) or
        (not on and ((false and reset) or
        (not reset and Flop(watchdog_is_on))))))
```

which obviously can be simplified into

```
watchdog_is_on = not RESET and
    (set or (not reset and Flop(watchdog_is_on)))
```

"Packing" operators into PABs

The next task concerns the expression of the resulting net of gates and flip-flops by means of PABs. The simplest way to perform this task consists in using one PAB for each operator in the net. Of course, this solution is very inefficient, but we will use it as a starting point. It is then improved by applying a set of packing rules. Figure 8.2(b) shows some of these rules, using the notations of Figure 8.2(a). The rules are applied according to some simple heuristics. For instance, the net that computes the variable watchdog_is_on (see Figure 8.3) may be packed into one PAB.

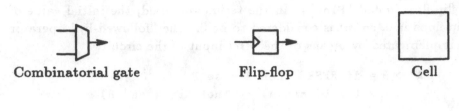

Combinatorial gate   Flip-flop   Cell

(a) Notations

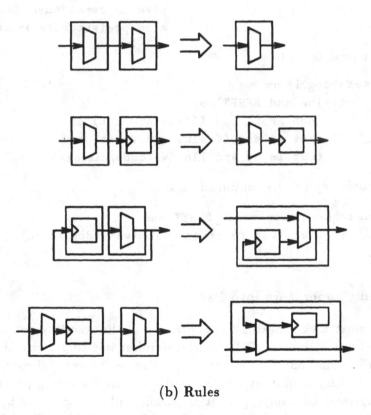

(b) Rules

Figure 8.2: Some rules for packing operators into PABs

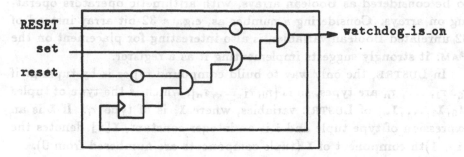

Figure 8.3: The cell computing the variable "watchdog_is_on"

8.2.3   Translating full Lustre

We have shown that the implementation of Boolean LUSTRE on the PAM is quite straightforward. If we want to deal with a larger subset of the language, we have to implement integer variables by vectors of bits. On the other hand, LUSTRE is a good candidate as a high-level language to program the PAM, but lacks some features concerning regular structures (arrays) and net geometry. Some extensions to the language have been proposed [RH91a, RH91b], which permit

- to deal with a greater subset of LUSTRE than the purely Boolean part. In particular, integers will be considered as vectors of bits.

- to make easier its use to describe circuits. Arrays will be available to describe regular structures. They will also carry placement informations.

Arrays in Lustre

Although they were considered in the very first design of the language, arrays have not yet been introduced in LUSTRE, since their translation to sequential code raises difficult problems concerning the order of computations. These problems disappear when a fully parallel implementation is considered. We propose here a notion of array, compatible with the principles of the language. Introducing arrays will allow integer values to be considered as Boolean arrays, with arithmetic operators operating on arrays. Considering a number as, e.g., a 32-bit array instead of 32 unrelated Boolean variables, is also interesting for placement on the PAM: it strongly suggests implementing it as a register.

In LUSTRE, the only way to build compound types is by tupling: if τ_0, τ_1, ..., τ_n are types, so is $[\tau_0, \tau_1, ..., \tau_n]$, which is the type of tuples $[X_0, X_1, ..., X_n]$ of LUSTRE variables, where X_i is of type τ_i. If X is an expression of type tuple and i is an integer constant, $X[i]$ denotes the $(i + 1)$th component of X (tuple components are numbered from 0).

The proposed notion of array is a special case of tuple. Let us define an *index* to be a nonnegative integer constant, known at compile time. If τ is a type and n is an index, then $\tau\texttt{\^{}}n$ is the type of arrays of n elements of type τ, numbered from 0 to n-1 (this notation refers to Cartesian power of τ). An array is a tuple, all components of which have the same type. As a consequence, if X is an array of type $\tau\texttt{\^{}}n$ and i is an index, $X[i]$ denotes the ith component of X (provided $0 \leq i < n$). One can also access a slice of an array: if X is as above and i and j are indexes smaller than n, then $X[i..j]$ is the array

- $[X[i], X[i+1], ..., X[j]]$ of type $\tau\texttt{\^{}}(j-i+1)$, if $i \leq j$

- $[X[i], X[i-1], ..., X[j]]$ of type $\tau\texttt{\^{}}(i-j+1)$, otherwise.

If $E_1, E_2, ..., E_n$ are expressions of the same type τ, then $[E_1, E_2, ..., E_n]$ denotes the array whose ith component is E_i. By extension, $E\texttt{\^{}}n$ denotes the array $[E, E, ..., E]$.

Of course, polymorphic LUSTRE operators can be applied to arrays. We introduce also the following notion of polymorphism: any operator op of the sort

$$\tau_1 \times \tau_2 \times ... \tau_i \rightarrow \tau_1' \times \tau_2' \times ... \tau_j'$$

(i.e., taking i parameters of respective types $\tau_1, \tau_2, ..., \tau_i$ and returning j results of respective types $\tau_1', \tau_2', ..., \tau_j'$) is implicitly overloaded to have the sort

$$\tau_1\texttt{\^{}}n \times \tau_2\texttt{\^{}}n \times ... \tau_i\texttt{\^{}}n \rightarrow \tau_1'\texttt{\^{}}n \times \tau_2'\texttt{\^{}}n \times ... \tau_j'\texttt{\^{}}n$$

for any index n. For instance, the operator and, of sort bool $\times$ bool $\rightarrow$ bool may be applied to two arrays A and B of type bool$\texttt{\^{}}$n, returning the array C such that C[i] = (A[i] and B[i]), for any i=0...n-1.

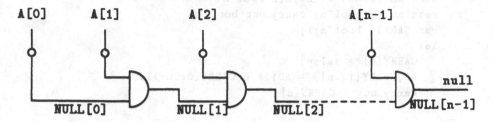

Figure 8.4: The net of the zero comparator

Implementing the full watchdog

We will translate the program WATCHDOG4 (see §6.2.2) into a Boolean program. First, we have to express arithmetic operators as operating on Boolean vectors. Let us give a comparator to zero and a combinatorial decrementer:

Zero comparator : It takes a vector of Booleans, representing an integer, together with its size, and returns *true* if and only if the represented integer is zero (see the resulting net in Figure 8.4):

```
node NULL(const n:int; A: bool^n) returns(null:bool);
var NULL: bool^n;
let
    null = NULL[n-1];
    NULL[1..n-1] = NULL[0..n-2] and not A[1..n-1];
    NULL[0] = not A[0];
tel;
```

Combinatorial decrementer: It is made of a general adder:

```
node DECR(const n:int; A:bool^n) returns (D:bool^n);
var carry_out:  bool;
let
    (S,carry_out) = ADD(n,A,true^n);
tel;
```

The n-bits adder is standard; it is made of n one-bit adders:

```
node ADD(const n:int;A,B:bool^n)
returns (S:bool^n; carry_out:bool);
var CARRY: bool^n+1;
let
    CARRY[0] = false;
    (S,CARRY[1..n]) = AD1(A,B,CARRY[0..n-1]);
    carry_out = CARRY[n];
tel;


node AD1(a,b,carry_in:  bool)
returns (s, carry_out:  bool);
let
    s = XOR(a, XOR(b,carry_in));
    carry_out = (a and b) or
                (b and carry_in) or (carry_in and a);
tel;
```

Full watchdog: Using these Boolean implementations of arithmetic operators, the watchdog program can be translated into a Boolean program. Here we choose an eight-bits representation of integers:

```
const size = 8;
type Int = bool^size;
node WATCHDOG4(set, reset, millisecond: bool; delay: Int)
    returns (alarm: bool);
var watchdog_is_on: bool; remaining_delay: Int;
let
    alarm = watchdog_is_on and NULL(size,remaining_delay);
    watchdog_is_on = false ->
            if set then true
            else if reset then false
            else pre(watchdog_is_on);
    remaining_delay =
            if set^size then delay
            else if (watchdog_is_on and millisecond)^size
            then DECR(size, pre(remaining_delay))
            else pre(remaining_delay);
tel;
```

The automatic translation of the initial program into this one is not yet implemented. However, a prototype silicon compiler, called POLLUX,

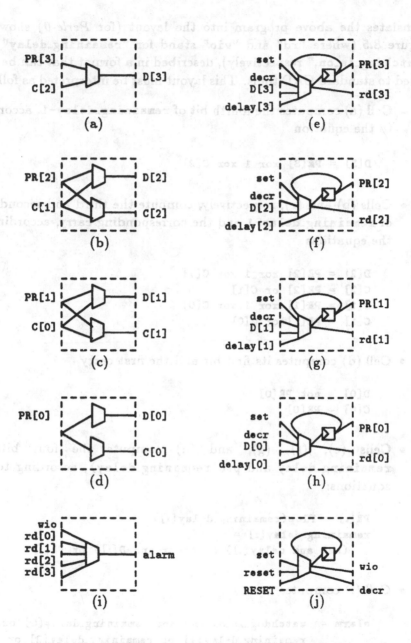

Figure 8.5: Layout of the watchdog on Perle-0

translates the above program into the layout (for *Perle-0*) shown in Figure 8.5 (where "rd" and "wio" stand for "remaining_delay" and "watchdog_is_on," respectively), described in a format that can be provided to standard CAD tools. This layout must be interpreted as follows:

- Cell (a) computes the fourth bit of remaining_delay-1, according to the equation

      D[3] = PR[3] xor 1 xor C[2]

- Cells (b) and (c), respectively, compute the third and second bits of remaining_delay-1 and the corresponding carry, according to the equations

      D[2] = PR[2] xor 1 xor C[1]
      C[2] = PR[2] or C[1]
      D[1] = PR[1] xor 1 xor C[0]
      C[1] = PR[1] or C[0]

- Cell (d) computes its first bit and the first carry

      D[0] = not PR[0]
      C[0] = PR[0]

- Cells (e), (f), (g), and (h) compute the four bits of remaining_delay and pre(remaining_delay), according to the equations:

      PR[i] = Flop(remaining_delay[i])
      remaining_delay[i] =
          (set and delay[i]) or (decr and D[i]) or PR[i]

- Cell (i) computes

      alarm = watchdog_is_on and not(remaining_delay[0] or
              remaining_delay[1] or remaining_delay[2] or
              remaining_delay[3])

- Cell (j) computes

```
watchdog_is_on = set or (not reset and not RESET and
                         Flop(watchdog_is_on))
decr = watchdog_is_on and millisecond
```

Its critical path is of about 60ns (much less than the time needed by a MC-68000 to perform a "load register" statement!).

8.3   Hardware implementation of pure Esterel

Implementing ESTEREL on hardware is much less obvious. The translation method is formally derived from ESTEREL behavioral semantics, and its correctness, which is not straightforward, is proven in [Ber91a]. The following intuitive presentation is essentially borrowed from the section 5 of [Ber91a].

8.3.1   Basic components

We here consider *pure* ESTEREL programs, i.e., programs handling pure signals only, without variables. The translation is structural. It results in a network of interconnected basic cells. There are five basic cells, which can be described in LUSTRE. In that sense, the translation can be viewed as a compilation of ESTEREL into LUSTRE. The basic cells are the following:

- The **Boot** cell has no input, and returns an output b, which is true at the initial instant, and always false afterward:

    ```
    b = true -> false;
    ```

- The **Halt** cell has two inputs c and r, and returns two outputs s and c' defined as follows:

    ```
    s = false -> pre(c and not r);
    c' = c;
    ```

- The Watch cell has three inputs a, c, and s, and returns three outputs a', c', and s':

      a' = c;
      c' = s and a
      s' = s;

- The Present cell has two inputs c and s and two outputs ct and cf:

      ct = c and s;
      cf = c and not s;

- Finally, a family of Parallel cells is defined, the Parallel[n] cell computing $n + 4$ outputs from its $n + 4$ inputs:

      s' = s;   a' = a;
      c' = c;   r' = r or c_2 or c_3 or ... or c_n
      c'_i = c_i and not(c_{i+1} or c_{i+2} or ... or c_n)

8.3.2   First example

Let us consider the following program:

```
module M:
input I, R;
output O;
loop
   loop
      await I ; await I; emit O
   end
each R.
```

After an initial instant when the input signals are ignored, it emits the signal O whenever it has received two occurrences of the input signal I, unless it is reset by an occurrence of R. Expanded into kernel statements, the body becomes

```
loop
   do
      loop
         do
            halt
         watching I;
         do
            halt
         watching I;
         emit O
      end
   watching R
end
```

The corresponding circuit is represented by Figure 8.6. Signals are represented by wires — which carry the value 1 (or *true*) at a given clock cycle, if and only if the corresponding signal occurs. The circuit contains three kinds of wires: the *selection* wires s0-s4, the *activation* wires a0-a4, and the *control* wires c0-c8. The unconnected pins of Halt cells are assumed to carry 0. Whenever two wires go to the same place, they are implicitly assumed to be combined by an or gate ("wired or").

The selection and activation wires go in reverse directions and form a tree, which is called the *skeleton* of the circuit. This tree is determined by the nesting of halt, watching, and parallel statements in the source program, as revealed by the source code indentation. The leftmost Halt and Watch cells correspond to the first await statement, the rightmost ones to the second await. The selection wires are used to determine which part of the circuit can be active in a given state: in our example, both await statements are in mutual exclusion, and one of them only can be active at a time. When the first await is active, the wires s2, s1, and s0 are on and select the leftmost branch of the tree. When the second await is active, the wires s4, s3, and s0 are on. The sources of the selection wires are the Halt cell registers.

The activation and control wires bear the flow of control. The activation wires handle preemption between watching statements.

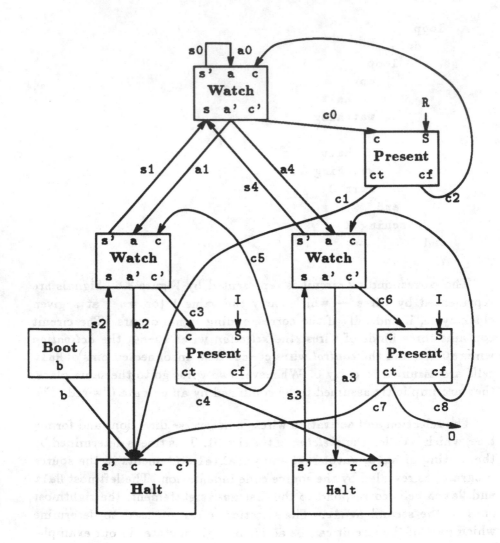

Figure 8.6: First circuit

A sample execution: At boot time, the Halt cell registers contain 0, and the selection wires are all 0. The boot control wire b is set and loads the leftmost Halt register.

On the next clock tick, assume that I is present and R is absent.

Then s2, s1, and s0 are set by the leftmost Halt register. The wires s0 and a0 being identical, the control flows down from a0 to c0 in order to test for R in the upper Present cell. Since R is not there, the control flows through the cf pin and sets c2, which is connected to the c pin of the upper Watch cell. This pin is directly connected to the activation wires a1 and a4. Since both s2 and a1 are on, the leftmost Watch cell sets c3 and the leftmost Present cell sets c4, since I is present. This loads the rightmost Halt register. Having no incoming control set, the leftmost Halt register is reset. This terminates the first "await I" statement.

On the next clock tick, if I is present, the execution is symmetrical: the rightmost Halt is reset and the leftmost one is set. The wires set to 1 are s3, s4, s0=a0, c0, c2, a1=a4, c6, and c7. Since c7 is also connected to the output O, this output is set. If instead R is present, the wires set are s3, s4,s0=a0, c0, and c1 which loads the leftmost Halt register, and one is back to the state just after boot. If no signal is present, the wires set are s3, s4,s0=a0, c0, c2, a1=a4, c6, c8, and a3, the rightmost Halt register is loaded, and the state is simply restored.

8.3.3 Translating Parallel and Exceptions

The most complex operator is, of course, the "parallel," since it must synchronize the termination of its branches and propagate exceptions. Consider the following program fragment:

```
trap T in
    await S
||
    present I then exit T end
end
```

The corresponding circuit fragment is shown in Figure 8.7. The leftmost Watch-Present-Halt cell group is generated by "await S." The rightmost Present cell is generated by "present I." The branches are simply put in parallel and synchronized by the Parallel cell. The circuit fragment starts when it receives control by the c0 wire.

The Parallel cell has two parts: the fork part, which involves the six leftmost pins, and the synchronization part, which involves the eight rightmost ones. The fork part is simple: selection wires are gathered, and

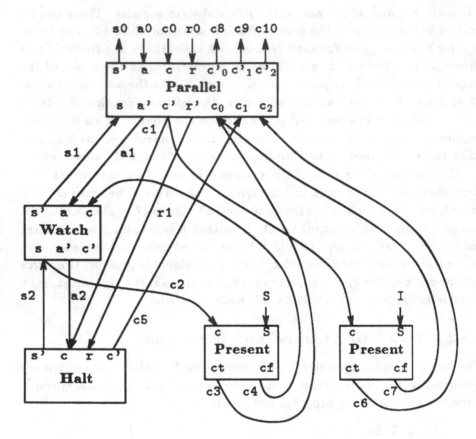

Figure 8.7: Second circuit

activation and control are dispatched to branches. The synchronization part is more subtle. A branch can stop in one of three cases (we will speak of *termination levels*):

(level 0) The branch terminates normally. In our example, the first branch normally terminates when S is present, and the second branch normally terminates when I is absent.

(level 1) The branch stops, waiting for a signal. In our example, the first branch stops, waiting for S when it is absent.

(level 2) The branch executes an "exit," like the second branch of our example, in the presence of I (in fact, we should consider $n + 2$ levels instead of three, for a process nested in n trap statements).

The basic observation is that the termination level of a "parallel" statement is the maximum termination level of its branches:

- If both branches normally terminate (level 0), so does the "parallel."

- If a branch stops and waits (level 1) and if the other does not execute an "exit" (level ≤ 1), then the "parallel" waits.

- If a branch executes an "exit" from a "trap" at n levels (level $n + 1$), the "parallel" is killed and performs the "exit."

The synchronization part of the Parallel cell computes this maximum level.

In our example, the left branch can halt, as signaled by wire c5, or terminate, as signaled by wire c3. The rightmost branch can terminate or exit T, as signaled by wires c7 and c6, respectively. According to the maximum termination level, the leftmost branch is killed by the wire r1 (which sends an inhibition signal to the Halt register), and the termination level is transmitted to the global context by means of wires c8, c9, and c10.

A sample execution: Assume that the circuit receives control by c0 and therefore sets c1. Then consider the following cases:

- Assume I is present. Then c5 is set by the Halt cell, and c6 is set by the right Present cell. The parallel cell selects the appropriate continuation c10 and inhibits the Halt register by setting r1.

- Assume instead that I is absent. Then c5 is set by the Halt cell and c5 is set by the right Present cell. The selected continuation is c9, which signals halting to the global context. Since the reset wire r1 is not set, the Halt cell register is loaded. The circuit remains in the same state as long as the activation wire a0 is set and S is not present: the wires set are s2, s1, s0, a1, c2, c4 a2, c5, and c9. If a0 remains high and S occurs, the wires set are s2, s1, s0, a1, c2, c3, and c8. The whole construct terminates and the register is reset, since c1 and a2 are low. The incoming activation wire a0 can also get down before S occurs, for instance because an enclosing watchdog elapses. Then the Halt register is also reset.

Optimization

Hardware experts will find that the obtained circuits are of very bad quality because of many useless gates and wires. This is because these circuits are obtained by a structural translation process, and there is much room for automatic optimization. Many wires are simply connected with each other; many logical functions are readily grouped by logic optimizers. Constant folding can also be used: for instance, the top activation wire is always set; using this fact, one can statically simplify many gates. Therefore, these circuits should be first treated by logic optimizers before actual implementation. For instance, optimizers based on Binary Decision Diagrams (BDD [Bry86]); see [BHSV90, CM90, STB91] drastically reduce the actual size of the circuit. They can also discover redundancies between registers and suppress some of them [BCM90a].

Let us reiterate that we have only tried here to provide an intuitive understanding about this translation from ESTEREL to circuits. The exact technique is more subtle (see [Ber91a]).

Part III

Program Verification

Chapter 9

Lustre program verification: the tool Lesar

As noted in the introduction, reactive systems often concern critical applications, and thus program verification is a key issue. However, many practitioners in the field are skeptical about the use of formal verification methods, and convincing arguments need to be provided in order to support the claim that such methods are indeed of practical interest. This is the object of the following discussion.

The research on program verification, which started in the early 1970s, intended to provide complete proofs of very general programs. Though this work has led to important contributions concerning programming techniques and language design, one should admit that its use is very limited in practice.

However, the goal concerning reactive systems may be less ambitious. Almost always, the safety of a critical application does not depend on the total correctness of its control program, but rather on an small set of properties that the program should fulfill. For instance, the occurrence of a critical situation should raise an alarm within a given delay. From our experience, the proof of such properties can often be handled within the framework of simple decidable theories, since these properties seldom depend on numerical relations and computations.

Furthermore, most of these properties are "safety" properties, which state that a given situation should never appear or that a given state-

139

ment should always hold, in contrast with "liveness" properties, which state that a given situation should eventually appear in the future.[1] For instance, a relevant question is not that a train will eventually stop, but that it will never cross a red light. This is an important point because proof techniques for safety properties are known to be much simpler than for liveness properties:

- A safety property can be checked on an abstraction of the actual program. Informally, if a safety property holds for a program, it also holds for programs whose set of behaviors is a subset of the initial one. Thus it is possible to abstract programs by ignoring details, for instance, numerical computations; their set of behaviors will become larger, and properties that hold on these abstractions will also hold on the actual programs.

- A safety property can be verified by simply checking properties of reachable states, instead of execution pathes. This allows the use of very efficient methods based on reachability [Hol87].

- Safety properties can be checked modularly. Properties of sub-modules can be combined so as to derive a property of the whole module. This allows proof complexities to be reduced, thanks to modular decomposition according to a program structure.

In view of this discussion, we will propose methods to specify and check simple safety properties about LUSTRE programs.

9.1   Specification of safety properties

Many formalisms have been proposed in order to express properties of real-time parallel programs. Two main approaches can be distinguished: those based on temporal logics (e.g., [Pnu77, MM84]), and those based on automata theory (Petri nets, STATECHARTS, timed graphs [ACD90], and process calculi [Mil83]).

Such formalisms should clearly allow any interesting property to be expressed, but they should also provide an easy and readable expression

---

[1] In fact, liveness properties often result from abstracting time from a real-time constraint. In a reactive system, time constraints are fully taken into account.

of it; proving a given property does not have much value if one cannot
be convinced that it is actually the desired property of the system!

From its declarative nature, LUSTRE appears to be also a good language to express properties of LUSTRE programs [HPOG89, RHR91].
This claim is based on the following arguments:

- LUSTRE can be considered as a subset of a temporal logic [PH88,
  BFH90]. The proposal is then to express any safety property P by
  a Boolean expression B, such that P holds if and only if expression
  B keeps holding *true* during any execution of the program. According to [BFH90], any safety property can be expressed in that
  way.

- The above proposal is easily implementable by using the assertion
  mechanism of LUSTRE: LUSTRE assertions are already a way to
  express properties of a program's environment.

- The use of a programming language to express both programs and
  their properties is interesting, since all the structuring facilities of
  the language become available for readability and expressiveness.
  For instance, as we will show, the node concept will allow the user
  to define its own temporal operators.

Let us show here how some useful nontrivial temporal operators can be
expressed as LUSTRE nodes. Consider the following property:

> "Any occurrence of a critical situation must be followed by
> an alarm within a five-second delay."

Such a property relates three events: the critical situation occurrence,
the alarm, and the deadline. The latter can be provided externally, and
it can also be easily expressed in LUSTRE. A general pattern for this
property is the following:

> "Any occurrence of event A is followed by an occurrence of
> event B before the next occurrence of event C."

However, this formulation is not directly translatable into LUSTRE, since
it refers to what happens in the future following an A occurrence, while
LUSTRE only allows references to the past with respect to the current

instant. That is why it is first translated into the equivalent past expression:

> "Anytime *C* occurs, either *A* has never occurred previously,
> or *B* has occurred since the last occurrence of *A*."

Let us define a node, taking three Boolean input parameters A, B, C, and returning a Boolean output X such that X is always true if and only if the property holds:

```
node onceBfromAtoC(A,B,C: bool) returns (X: bool);
let
    X = implies(C, never(A) or since(B,A))
tel
```

The equation defining X uses three auxiliary nodes:

- The node **implies** implements the ordinary logical implication:

  ```
  node implies(A, B: bool) returns (AimpliesB: bool);
  let AimpliesB = not A or B tel
  ```

- The node **never** returns the value *true* as long as its input has never been equal to *true*. Then it returns *false* forever:

  ```
  node never(B: bool) returns (neverB: bool);
  let
      neverB = (not B) -> (not B and pre(neverB))
  tel
  ```

- Finally, the node **since** has two inputs, and it returns *true* if and only if either its second input has still not been *true*, or its first input has been *true* at least once since the last *true* value of the second input:

  ```
  node since(X,Y: bool) returns (XsinceY: bool);
  let
      XsinceY = if Y then X
                else (true -> X or pre(XsinceY))
  tel
  ```

A realistic example has been studied in [Glo89]: most critical properties of a nuclear plant monitoring program have been expressed in LUSTRE, thanks to a small set of general purpose temporal operators similar to "onceBfromAtoC," "never" or "since."

9.2   Verification

The proposed verification method is very similar to "model checking" [CES86, RRSV87]: first, the state graph of the program is built (this obviously assumes a finite number of states), and then each property is checked on this state graph. The critical issue in this approach is clearly the number of states, which can be very large for realistic programs. We will see that the restriction to safety properties, and the expression of properties in the same language as the program, may help in solving this problem.

In the LUSTRE case, a state graph already exists corresponding to the control automaton built by the compiler. This graph is an abstraction of the actual state graph, since it only expresses the control and ignores many details concerning non-Boolean variables and Boolean variables that do not influence that control. As noticed above, if properties to be checked essentially depend on Booleans taken into account in the control graph, and if these properties are safety ones, such an abstraction is a sensible one for checking purposes and generally yields much smaller graphs.

An important observation to decrease the total graph size consists in taking into account the property to be checked when building the state graph. In the case of LUSTRE this is easily achieved, since the same language applies to properties and programs: in order to prove that an expression B is an invariant of the program P, we build a new program P' made of the body of P and of the system of equations defining B, and whose only output is B (cf. Figure 9.1). Since the compiler is then only requested to compute B, it will only take into account the part of the program concerning that computation, and this can be expected to yield a smaller graph. Given that graph, verifying the property corresponds to checking that in none of the states does the code perform an assignment of the output to *false*.

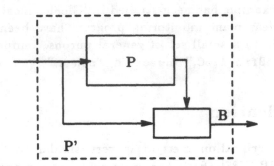

Figure 9.1: Verification program

A third issue in reducing the size of the graph consists in using assertions to express assumptions under which the property is intended to hold. Assertions are also useful to express properties of numbers that would otherwise be ignored by the compiler. For instance, if a program uses numerical tests such as X<=Z and Y<=Z, the assertion

assert implies(X<=Y and Y<=Z, X<=Z);

prevents the compiler from generating states satisfying $Z<X\leq Y\leq Z$, which of course would not be reachable by the actual program.

As an example, let us consider the following general purpose node,[2] which represents a switch: its output alternates from *true* to *false* according to input events ON and OFF; a third input defines its initial value. A first version of this node could be

```
node SWITCH_1(ON, OFF, INIT: bool) returns (STATE: bool);
let
    STATE = INIT -> if ON then true
                    else if OFF then false
                    else pre(STATE);
tel.
```

---

[2]Such a node could have been used in defining the variable watchdog_in_on in the WATCHDOG programs, and in defining the states of the STOPWATCH.

However, this version has a flaw: in the call

```
state = SWITCH_1(button, button, init)
```

the output does not change each time the button is pushed, as we might expect. Thus a more general version should take into account the previous STATE when checking the inputs ON and OFF:

```
node SWITCH(ON, OFF, INIT: bool) returns (STATE: bool);
let
    STATE = INIT -> if ON and not pre(STATE) then true
                    else if OFF and pre(STATE) then false
                    else pre(STATE);
tel.
```

We could wish to verify that this generalization is correct, in the sense that both versions behave in the same way as long as the inputs ON and OFF are never true at the same time. This is achieved by constructing a comparison node that calls both nodes with the same inputs and compares their outputs, under the assumption that ON and OFF inputs are exclusive (cf. Figure 9.2):

```
node COMPARE(ON, OFF, INIT: bool) returns (OK: bool);
var state, state_1 : bool;
let
    state = SWITCH(ON, OFF, INIT);
    state_1 = SWITCH_1(ON, OFF, INIT);
    OK = (state = state_1);
    assert not(ON and OFF);
tel.
```

Compiling this node yields a five-state automaton, each transition of which assigns the value *true* to the output OK.

The last way to tackle the state explosion problem is *modular verification*. Having to prove that an expression B is always true during the execution of a program P calling a node Q (cf. Figure 9.3(a)), the idea is to decompose the proof into a subproof concerning Q and a subproof concerning P without Q:

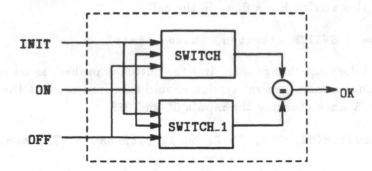

Figure 9.2: Assumption-dependent equivalence of programs

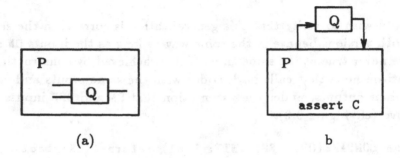

(a)   b

Figure 9.3: Modular verification

- Find (by intuition) a property of Q, i.e., an expression C on the input/output parameters of Q, and prove that C is always true during any execution of Q.

- Now, consider Q as being part of the environment of P, i.e., replace in P the call to Q by the assertion **assert C**. Then try to prove the invariance of B on the modified program (cf. Figure 9.3(b)).

An example making use of this modular decomposition may be found in [HL90].

A prototype verification tool called LESAR (by analogy with the CESAR family of model checkers) has been implemented: given a program with a single Boolean output, it goes through the states and checks that the output is never assigned *false*. If such a situation is found, a diagnostic is provided. Otherwise, LESAR concludes that the property is satisfied. In fact, two "verification engines" are available:

- The first engine explicitly enumerates the reachable states, as done by standard model checkers [CES86, QS82]. The main limitation of such an approach is obviously the number of states that can be considered. The present version of the tool deals with programs of about one million states in a reasonable time (less than one hour).

- The second engine proceeds symbolically: starting from a Boolean formula F_0, characterizing the set of states where the output is *true*, it iteratively computes a sequence $F_1, F_2, \ldots, F_n$ of formulas, where F_{i+1} characterizes the set of states, belonging to F_i and necessarily leading (in one execution step) into F_i. As soon as the initial state does not satisfy F_i, we can conclude that the property is not satisfied, since there exists an execution path leading to a state where the output is *false*. Otherwise, since the state space is finite, the sequence of formulas converges after a finite number of steps. Our tool performs symbolic computations over formulas using *binary decision diagrams* [Bry86], a compact canonical encoding of Boolean formulas. This approach is sometimes called "symbolic model checking" [BCM+90b, CBM89, CMB90].

The two approaches are complementary: in some cases, the enumerative method is more efficient than the symbolic one, and conversely.

Of course, the validity of the proof relies on the satisfaction of the synchrony hypothesis: the whole proof is performed "inside" the synchronous model, and has nothing to do with performance analysis. As mentioned before, checking the validity of the synchrony hypothesis amounts to evaluate the maximum reaction time of the program on a given machine.

Chapter 10

Using Auto for Esterel program verification

Another approach to program verification, also based on automata, has been applied to ESTEREL. It starts from the statement that program specification is a difficult task, almost as error-prone as program writing. The basic idea, therefore, is not to write a specification, but rather simply to observe the behavior of the generated automaton. Of course, a complete automaton cannot be manually analyzed; even a small automaton, of about ten states, can be quite complex. The proposed approach offers *reduction methods*, providing partial views on the automaton, on which one can easily detect anomalies and check properties. The verification tool AUTO [Ver86, BRdSV90, RdS90] has been developed at INRIA, in order to perform such reductions. The graphic editor AUTOGRAPH [RS89, Roy90] allows (reduced) automata to be visualized.

The main goal of AUTO is automaton reduction. These reductions preserve some semantic properties. They are based on process calculus and mainly use the notions of *bisimulation* and *observation criteria* [Mil80].

Let us illustrate this approach for synchronous program verification by means of a simple example borrowed from [BS91]. This example is an ESTEREL program implementing a lift controller. The full automaton produced by ESTEREL compilation is shown on Figure 10.1 in its AUTOGRAPH postscript output. Each transition corresponds to a pro-

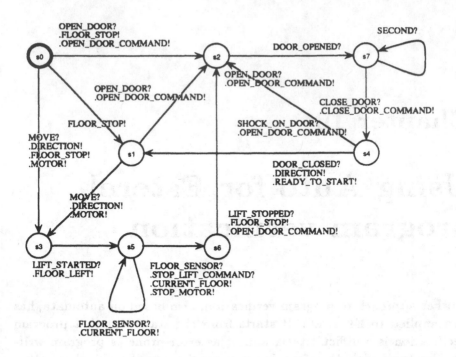

Figure 10.1: The full automaton of a lift controller

gram reaction. Transitions are labeled by received (S?) and emitted (S!) signals.

Now, assume we want to check that the lift cannot move while the door is open. Even for such a simple program, the automaton is rather complex and this property is not obvious. For the considered property, the only relevant signals are the input signals LIFT_STOPPED and DOOR_CLOSED and the output signals OPEN_DOOR_COMMAND and MOTOR. In order to observe the behavior of the automaton with respect to these signals, AUTO first renames any other signal by the same "dummy" name, which is usually denoted by τ. The resulting simplified automaton is given by Figure 10.2.

The automaton reduction then consists in considering some states as being equivalent. Of course, the choice of a "good" equivalence relation is critical: the coarser it is, the most effective the reduction is, but if

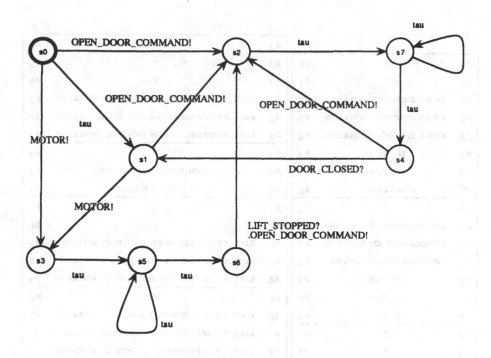

Figure 10.2: Simplified automaton

it is too coarse, it may not preserve some properties. Here, we will use the *observational congruence*, whose construction is illustrated now. Reducing an automaton according to this relation consists of two steps:

- The "τ-saturation" aims at assimilating any sequence of transitions $(\xrightarrow{\tau})^* \xrightarrow{a} (\xrightarrow{\tau})^*$ — made of some dummy transitions, followed by a significant transition, followed by some dummy transitions — with the significant transition $\xrightarrow{a}$. This is made by adding transitions to the automaton. The result in our example is shown by the transition table 10.1.

- The "τ-saturated" automaton is then reduced by bisimulation. We detail this second step below.

Let $A = (S, L, \rightarrow)$ be an automaton, where S is a set of states, L is a set of labels, and $\rightarrow$ is a transition relation included in $S \times L \times S$. Let

				s_3	τ	s_3
s_0	τ	s_0		s_3	τ	s_5
s_0	τ	s_1		s_3	τ	s_6
s_0	OPEN_DOOR_COMMAND!	s_2		s_3	LIFT_STOPPED?OPEN_DOOR_COMMAND!	s_2
s_0	OPEN_DOOR_COMMAND!	s_7		s_3	LIFT_STOPPED?OPEN_DOOR_COMMAND!	s_7
s_0	OPEN_DOOR_COMMAND!	s_4		s_3	LIFT_STOPPED?OPEN_DOOR_COMMAND!	s_4
s_0	MOTOR!	s_3		s_4	τ	s_4
s_0	MOTOR!	s_5		s_4	OPEN_DOOR_COMMAND!	s_2
s_0	MOTOR!	s_6		s_4	DOOR_CLOSED?	s_1
s_1	τ	s_1		s_5	τ	s_5
s_1	OPEN_DOOR_COMMAND!	s_2		s_5	τ	s_6
s_1	OPEN_DOOR_COMMAND!	s_7		s_5	LIFT_STOPPED?OPEN_DOOR_COMMAND!	s_2
s_1	OPEN_DOOR_COMMAND!	s_4		s_5	LIFT_STOPPED?OPEN_DOOR_COMMAND!	s_7
s_1	MOTOR!	s_3		s_5	LIFT_STOPPED?OPEN_DOOR_COMMAND!	s_4
s_1	MOTOR!	s_5		s_6	τ	s_6
s_1	MOTOR!	s_6		s_6	LIFT_STOPPED?OPEN_DOOR_COMMAND!	s_2
s_2	τ	s_2		s_6	LIFT_STOPPED?OPEN_DOOR_COMMAND!	s_7
s_2	τ	s_7		s_6	LIFT_STOPPED?OPEN_DOOR_COMMAND!	s_4
s_2	τ	s_4		s_7	τ	s_7
s_2	OPEN_DOOR_COMMAND!	s_2		s_7	τ	s_4
s_2	DOOR_CLOSED?	s_1		s_7	OPEN_DOOR_COMMAND!	s_2
				s_7	DOOR_CLOSED?	s_1

Table 10.1: Transition table of the τ-saturated automaton

us recall that a relation $\approx$ among the states of A is a bisimulation if and only if $\forall s_1, s_2 \in S$,

$$s_1 \approx s_2 \iff$$
$$\forall s_1' \text{ such that } s_1 \xrightarrow{a} s_1', \quad \exists s_2' \approx s_1' \text{ such that } s_2 \xrightarrow{a} s_2'$$
$$\text{and} \quad \forall s_2' \text{ such that } s_2 \xrightarrow{a} s_2', \quad \exists s_1' \approx s_2' \text{ such that } s_1 \xrightarrow{a} s_1'$$

The reduction of A according to a bisimulation $\approx$ is the automaton $A/\approx \; = (S/\approx, L, \rightarrow)$, whose states are equivalence classes of $\approx$, and such that, $\forall C_1, C_2 \in S/\approx$,

$$C_1 \xrightarrow{a} C_2 \text{ iff } \exists s_1 \in C_1, \exists s_2 \in C_2 \text{ such that } s_1 \xrightarrow{a} s_2$$

s_0	τ	C_0^0
s_0	OPEN_DOOR_COMMAND!	C_0^0
s_0	MOTOR!	C_0^0
s_1	τ	C_0^0
s_1	OPEN_DOOR_COMMAND!	C_0^0
s_1	MOTOR!	C_0^0
s_2	τ	C_0^0
s_2	OPEN_DOOR_COMMAND!	C_0^0
s_2	DOOR_CLOSED?	C_0^0
s_3	τ	C_0^0
s_3	LIFT_STOPPED? OPEN_DOOR_COMMAND!	C_0^0

s_4	τ	C_0^0
s_4	OPEN_DOOR_COMMAND!	C_0^0
s_4	DOOR_CLOSED?	C_0^0
s_5	τ	C_0^0
s_5	LIFT_STOPPED? OPEN_DOOR_COMMAND!	C_0^0
s_6	τ	C_0^0
s_6	LIFT_STOPPED? OPEN_DOOR_COMMAND!	C_0^0
s_7	τ	C_0^0
s_7	OPEN_DOOR_COMMAND!	C_0^0
s_7	DOOR_CLOSED?	C_0^0

Table 10.2: Result of the first reduction step

The reduction of an automaton according to the coarsest bisimulation is a well-known problem, and efficient algorithms have been proposed for its construction [AHU74, PT87]. For simplicity, we apply here a straightforward algorithm. We will build a sequence $(\rho_0, \rho_1, \ldots, \rho_n, \ldots)$ of equivalence relations as follows:

- ρ_0 is the trivial equivalence (all the states are equivalent).

- Let $\{C_0^n, C_1^n, \ldots, C_k^n\}$ be the equivalence classes of ρ_n. We note by $s \xrightarrow{a} C_i^n$ the fact that there exists s' in C_i^n such that $s \xrightarrow{a} s'$. The relation ρ_{n+1} is defined from ρ_n as follows:

$$(s_1, s_2) \in \rho_{n+1} \quad \Longleftrightarrow \quad \forall a \in L, \forall C_i^n, \ s_1 \xrightarrow{a} C_i^n \text{ iff } s_2 \xrightarrow{a} C_i^n$$

The algorithm stops when $\rho_n = \rho_{n+1}$. In our example the following iterations take place:

- Initially, all the states are considered equivalent. Let C_0^0 be the unique equivalence class. All the transitions are thus considered to lead to C_0^0. The transition table is given by Table 10.2. In this

s_0	τ	C_0^1
s_0	OPEN_DOOR_COMMAND!	C_1^1
s_0	MOTOR!	C_2^1
s_1	τ	C_0^1
s_1	OPEN_DOOR_COMMAND!	C_1^1
s_1	MOTOR!	C_2^1
s_2	τ	C_1^1
s_2	OPEN_DOOR_COMMAND!	C_1^1
s_2	DOOR_CLOSED?	C_0^1
s_3	τ	C_2^1
s_3	LIFT_STOPPED? OPEN_DOOR_COMMAND!	C_1^1

s_4	τ	C_1^1
s_4	OPEN_DOOR_COMMAND!	C_1^1
s_4	DOOR_CLOSED?	C_0^1
s_5	τ	C_2^1
s_5	LIFT_STOPPED? OPEN_DOOR_COMMAND!	C_1^1
s_6	τ	C_2^1
s_6	LIFT_STOPPED? OPEN_DOOR_COMMAND!	C_1^1
s_7	τ	C_1^1
s_7	OPEN_DOOR_COMMAND!	C_1^1
s_7	DOOR_CLOSED?	C_0^1

Table 10.3: Result of the second reduction step

table, three classes obviously appear (the states of a given class have the same outgoing transitions):

$$C_0^1 = \{s_0, s_1\} , \ C_1^1 = \{s_2, s_4, s_7\} , \ C_2^1 = \{s_3, s_5, s_6\}$$

- Replacing, in the initial transition table, each target state by the unique class to which it belongs, we get Table 10.3, which gives the same classes as before. All the states belonging to a given class have the same outgoing transitions. The algorithm has converged, and we have the classes of the coarsest bisimulation.

The result of the reduction is given in Figure 10.3. In this figure, the property is obvious if we assume that

- the door is initially closed;

- the door can only be opened between an emission of OPEN_DOOR_COMMAND and the next reception of DOOR_CLOSED; and

- the lift can only be moving between an emission of MOTOR and the next reception of LIFT_STOPPED.

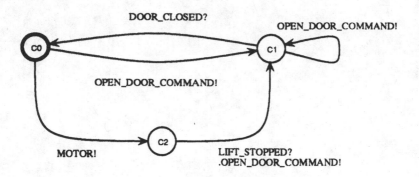

Figure 10.3: Reduced automaton

Chapter 11

Conclusion

The ESTEREL, LUSTRE, and SIGNAL compilers are now commercial products (see the industrial contacts given in the Foreword). The industrialization of ARGOS will start soon.

As a conclusion, we will present an ongoing project that aims at normalizing a common environment for synchronous languages, and we will outline some works in progress and perspectives.

11.1 The common environment of synchronous languages

In Section 6.3, we have presented the common tools developed around ESTEREL and LUSTRE and presently used also by ARGOS through the IC format. A more ambitious ongoing project concerns a common environment to be used by all the synchronous languages. This project consists of defining and normalizing a set of common formats on which many tools of general usage will be connected. Experiences with IC and OC show that this goal is more realistic than defining a single common format. As a matter of fact, to minimize the translation effort from source languages to a common format, we were led to distinguish a format well suited to imperative languages (an extension of IC is under normalization) and a format adapted to declarative languages (this new format will be called GC, for "graph code") on which specific tools will be available. A translator from IC to GC, called icgc, will be built,

157

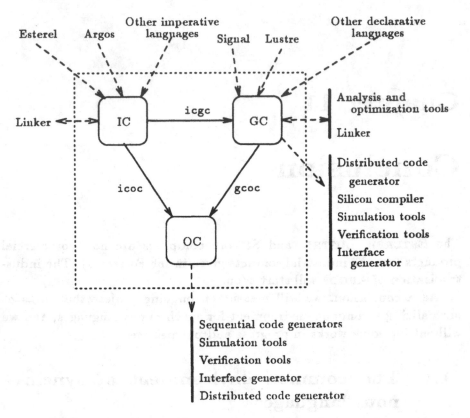

Figure 11.1: The common environment of synchronous languages

which is inspired from the hardware implementation of ESTEREL. So IC and GC form the input level of the environment. At a low level, the OC code will be used as a target format for sequential code. Two compilers to this code will remain, one from IC (which corresponds to the present icoc module of the ESTEREL compiler) and one from GC, since the automaton generation from declarative languages needs the minimization of the target automaton [HRR91].

The projected environment is pictured in Figure 11.1. An important goal of this project is to permit several modules, written in various languages, to be interfaced at the internal formats level.

11.2   Works in progress

In addition to this common project, some extensions to each language are under investigation (some of them are already implemented):

Asynchronous tasks in ESTEREL: A new primitive is being added to ESTEREL [Par92, AMP92] that allows external asynchronous tasks to be called from an ESTEREL program. The statement "exec T" launches the external task T and waits for its termination. Nontrivial problems arise because of the interactions of this new statement with the interruption mechanisms provided by the language: when a program fragment running an external task is interrupted, the task must be killed *if it is not already terminated.* Moreover, several instances of the same task can run at the same time, and the suitable instance only must be killed. Many applications of this mechanism have been identified, e.g., in robotics [CM91].

Adding actions to ARGOS: Some work remains to be done in order to make ARGOS a full programming language. Obviously, an ARGOS program must be able to handle variables and to perform actions on them. Until now, emphasis has been placed on specific control structures, but the data part will be readily added to the language.

Arrays in LUSTRE: We have seen in §8.2.3 that an array mechanism has been added to LUSTRE in order to describe regular hardware devices. This mechanism is being inserted in the standard language, but its compilation must be further studied: it is presently performed by "macro-expansion," by associating a variable with each array element. Compiling LUSTRE arrays into real arrays raises many problems concerning causality checking and finding the right computation order.

Randomized SIGNAL: An probabilistic extension of SIGNAL is under investigation [Ben91], which takes advantage of the fact that SIGNAL allows the description of nondeterministic systems. The idea is to restrict this nondeterminism by means of probabilistic laws. Applications concern fault-tolerant systems and simulation of random processes.

Bibliography

[ACD90]   R. Alur, C. Courcoubetis, and D. Dill. Model checking of real-time systems. In *Fifth IEEE Symposium on Logic in Computer Science, Philadelphia*, 1990.

[ADA83]   ADA. *The Programming Language* ADA *Reference Manual*, *LNCS 155*. Springer Verlag, 1983.

[AHU74]   A. Aho, J. Hopcroft, and J. Ullman. *Design and analysis of computer Algorithms*. Addison Wesley, 1974.

[AMP92]   C. André, J.P. Marmorat, and J.P. Paris. Execution machines for Esterel. In *1st European Control Conference, Grenoble*, July 1992.

[AW85]   E. A. Ashcroft and W. W. Wadge. LUCID, *the data-flow programming language*. Academic Press, 1985.

[BBB89]   R. Bernhard, G. Berry, and F. Boussinot. The OCC c generated code interface manual. Technical Report Ecole Nationale Supérieure des Mines de Paris, December 1989.

[BC85]   M. C. Browne and E. M. Clarke. SML — a high-level language for the design and verification of finite state machines. Research Report CMU-CS-85-179, Carnegie Mellon University, 1985.

[BCG87]   G. Berry, P. Couronné, and G. Gonthier. Programmation synchrone des systèmes réactifs , le langage ESTEREL. *Technique et Science Informatique*, 4:305–316, 1987.

161

[BCG88]   G. Berry, P. Couronné, and G. Gonthier. Synchronous pro-
            gramming of reactive systems, an introduction to ESTEREL.
            In K. Fuchi and M. Nivat, editors, *Programming of Future
            Generation Computers.* Elsevier Science Publisher B.V.
            (North Holland), 1988. INRIA Report 647.

[BCH⁺85]   J-L. Bergerand, P. Caspi, N. Halbwachs, D. Pilaud, and
            E. Pilaud. Outline of a real-time data-flow language. In
            1985 Real-Time Symposium, San Diego, December 1985.

[BCHP86]   J-L. Bergerand, P. Caspi, N. Halbwachs, and J. Plaice.
            Automatic control systems programming using a real-time
            declarative language. In *IFAC/IFIP Symp. 'SOCOCO 86,
            Graz*, May 1986.

[BCM90a]   C. Berthet, O. Coudert, and J. C. Madre. New ideas on
            symbolic manipulations of finite state machines. In *Inter-
            national Conference on Computer Design (ICCD), Cam-
            bridge*, September 1990.

[BCM⁺90b]   J.R. Burch, E.M. Clarke, K.L. McMillan, D.L. Dill, and
            J. Hwang. Symbolic model checking: 10^{20} states and be-
            yond. In *Fifth IEEE Symposium on Logic in Computer
            Science, Philadelphia*, 1990.

[BCP88]   B. Buggiani, P. Caspi, and D. Pilaud. Programming dis-
            tributed automatic control systems: a language and com-
            piler solution. Technical Report SPECTRE L4, IMAG,
            Grenoble, July 1988.

[Ben91]   A. Benveniste. Constructive probability and the SIG-
            NALEA language: building and handling stochastic pro-
            cesses via programming. RR 1532, INRIA, 1991.

[Ber89]   G. Berry. Real time programming: Special purpose or gen-
            eral purpose languages. In *IFIP World Computer Congress,
            San Francisco*, 1989.

[Ber91a]   G. Berry. A hardware implementation of pure ESTEREL. In *ACM Workshop on Formal Methods in VLSI Design, Miami*, January 1991.

[Ber91b]   G. Berry. Programming a digital watch in ESTEREL v3_2. Technical Report 08/91, Centre de Mathématiques Appliquées, Ecole des Mines de Paris, Sophia-Antipolis, 1991.

[BFH90]   A. Bouajjani, J. C. Fernandez, and N. Halbwachs. On the verification of safety properties. Technical Report SPECTRE L12, IMAG, Grenoble, March 1990.

[BFH+92]   A. Bouajjani, J. C. Fernandez, N. Halbwachs, P. Raymond, and C. Ratel. Minimal state graph generation. *Science of Computer Programming*, 18:247–269, 1992.

[BG88]   G. Berry and G. Gonthier. The synchronous programming language ESTEREL, design, semantics, implementation. Technical Report 842, INRIA, 1988. *To appear in Science of Computer Programming*.

[BHSV90]   R. K. Brayton, G. D. Hachtel, and A. L. Sangiovanni-Vincentelli. Multilevel logic synthesis. *Proceedings of the IEEE*, 78(2), 1990.

[BL85]   D. Borrione and C. Le Faou. Overview of the CASCADE multilevel hardware description language and its mixed mode simulation mechanisms. In *Computer Hardware Description Languages and Their Applications*. Elsevier Science, North Holland, 1985.

[BL90]   A. Benveniste and P. LeGuernic. Hybrid dynamical systems theory and the SIGNAL language. *IEEE Transactions on Automatic Control*, 35(5):535–546, May 1990.

[Bou91]   F. Boussinot. Programming a reflex game in Esterel v3_2. Research Report 07/91, Centre de Mathématiques Appliquées, Ecole des Mines de Paris, Sophia-Antipolis, 1991.

[BRdSV90]   G. Boudol, V. Roy, R. de Simone, and D. Vergamini. Process calculi, from theory to practice: Verification tools. In *International Workshop on Automatic Verification Methods for Finite State Systems, Grenoble, LNCS 407*. Springer Verlag, 1990.

[Bro89]   M. Broy. Functional specification of time sensitive communicating systems. In REX *Workshop*, 1989.

[BRV90]   P. Bertin, D. Roncin, and J. Vuillemin. Introduction to programmable active memories. In J. McCanny, J. McWhirter, and E. Swartzlander, editors, *Systolic Array Processors*. Prentice-Hall, 1990.

[Bry86]   R. E. Bryant. Graph-based algorithms for boolean function manipulation. *IEEE Transactions on Computers*, C-35(8):677–692, 1986.

[Brz64]   J. A. Brzozowski. Derivative of regular expressions. *JACM*, 11(4), 1964.

[BS87]   G. Berry and R. Sethi. From regular expressions to deterministic automata. *TCS*, 25(1), 1987.

[BS91]   F. Boussinot and R. de Simone. The ESTEREL language. *Proceedings of the IEEE*, 79(9):1293–1304, September 1991.

[CBM89]   O. Coudert, C. Berthet, and J. C. Madre. Verification of synchronous sequential machines based on symbolic execution. In *International Workshop on Automatic Verification Methods for Finite State Systems, Grenoble, LNCS 407*. Springer Verlag, 1989.

[CES86]   E. M. Clarke, E. A. Emerson, and A. P. Sistla. Automatic verification of finite-state concurrent systems using temporal logic specifications. *ACM TOPLAS*, 8(2), 1986.

[CM90]   O. Coudert and J. C. Madre. A unified framework for the formal verification of sequential circuits. In *International Conference on Computer Aided Design (ICCAD), Santa Clara*, 1990.

[CM91]   E. Coste-Manière. Synchronisme et asynchronisme dans la programmation des systèmes robotiques: apport du langage Esterel et de concepts objets. Thesis, Ecole Nationale Supérieure des Mines de Paris, 1991.

[CMB90]   O. Coudert, J. C. Madre, and C. Berthet. Verifying temporal properties of sequential machines without building their state diagrams. In R. Kurshan, editor, *International Workshop on Computer Aided Verification, Rutgers*, June 1990.

[Cou90]   Ph. Couronné. Le système ESTEREL v2. Thesis, Université Paris VII, December 1990.

[CPHP87]   P. Caspi, D. Pilaud, N. Halbwachs, and J. Plaice. LUSTRE: a declarative language for programming synchronous systems. In *14th ACM Symposium on Principles of Programming Languages, Munchen*, January 1987.

[Fer90]   J. C. Fernandez. An implementation of an efficient algorithm for bisimulation equivalence. *Science of Computer Programming*, 13(2-3), May 1990.

[GGB87]   T. Gauthier, P. Le Guernic, and L. Besnard. Signal, a declarative language for synchronous programming of real-time systems. In *Proc. 3rd. Conf. on Functional Programming Languages and Computer Architecture, LNCS 274*. Springer Verlag, 1987.

[Ghe92]   G. Gherardi. Sahara: un environnement de mise au point graphique pour les programmes Esterel (in Preparation). Thesis, Université de Nice, 1992.

[Glo89]   A-C. Glory. Vérification de propriétés de programmes flots de données synchrones. Thesis, Université Joseph Fourier, Grenoble, December 1989.

[GMP+90]   N. Ghezal, S. Matiatos, P. Piovezan, Y. Sorel, and M. Sorine. SYNDEX, un environnement de programmation pour multi-processeur de traitement du signal. Mécanismes de communication. Technical Report 1236, INRIA Rocquencourt, France, 1990.

[Gon85]   G. Gonthier. Private communication. 1985.

[Gon88]   G. Gonthier. Sémantiques et modèles d'exécution des langages réactifs synchrones; application à ESTEREL. Thesis, University of Paris VI, 1988.

[Gra82]   J. R. Mc Graw. The VAL language: Description and analysis. *ACM TOPLAS*, 4(1), January 1982.

[Har87]   D. Harel. Statecharts: A visual approach to complex systems. *Science of Computer Programming*, 8(3), 1987.

[HCRP91]   N. Halbwachs, P. Caspi, P. Raymond, and D. Pilaud. The synchronous dataflow programming language LUSTRE. *Proceedings of the IEEE*, 79(9):1305–1320, September 1991.

[HGd88]   C. Huizing, R. Gerth, and W. P. de Roever. Modelling Statecharts behaviour in a fully abstract way. In *13th CAAP, LNCS 299*. Springer Verlag, 1988.

[HL90]   N. Halbwachs and F. Lagnier. An experience in proving regular networks of processes by modular model checking. Technical Report SPECTRE L13 (to appear in Acta Informatica), IMAG, Grenoble, March 1990.

[Hol87]   G. J. Holzmann. On limits and possibilities of automated protocols analysis. In *IFIP WG-6.1 7th. International Conference on Protocol Specification, Testing and Verification*. North Holland, 1987.

[HP85]   D. Harel and A. Pnueli. On the development of reactive systems. In *Logic and Models of Concurrent Systems, NATO Advanced Study Institute on Logics and Models for Verification and Specification of Concurrent Systems*. Springer Verlag, 1985.

[HPOG89]   N. Halbwachs, D. Pilaud, F. Ouabdesselam, and A.C. Glory. Specifying, programming and verifying real-time systems, using a synchronous declarative language. In *Workshop on Automatic Verification Methods for Finite State Systems, Grenoble, LNCS 407*. Springer Verlag, June 1989.

[HPSS86]   D. Harel, A. Pnueli, J. P. Schmidt, and R. Sherman. On the formal semantics of Statecharts. In *Logic in Computer Science*, 1986.

[HRR91]   N. Halbwachs, P. Raymond, and C. Ratel. Generating efficient code from data-flow programs. In *Third International Symposium on Programming Language Implementation and Logic Programming*, Passau, August 1991.

[INM84]   INMOS Ltd. *The Occam Programming Manual*. Prentice-Hall International, 1984.

[Kah74]   G. Kahn. The semantics of a simple language for parallel programming. In *IFIP 74*. North Holland, 1974.

[KQ77]   G. Kahn and D. B. Mac Queen. Coroutines and networks of parallel processes. In *IFIP Congress*, 1977.

[LBBG85]   P. LeGuernic, A. Benveniste, P. Bournai, and T. Gautier. SIGNAL: a data-flow oriented language for signal processing. RR 378, INRIA, 1985.

[LeG89]   B. LeGoff. Inférence de contrôle hiérarchique, application au temps réel. Thesis, Université Rennes 1, June 1989.

[LGLL91]   P. LeGuernic, T. Gautier, M. LeBorgne, and C. LeMaire. Programming real time applications with SIGNAL. *Proceedings of the IEEE*, 79(9):1321–1336, September 1991.

[Mar89]   F. Maraninchi. Argonaute: graphical description, semantics and verification of reactive systems by using a process algebra. In *International Workshop on Automatic Verification Methods for Finite State Systems, Grenoble, LNCS 407*. Springer Verlag, 1989.

[Mar90]   F. Maraninchi. Argos, un langage graphique pour la con-
           ception, la description et la validation des systèmes réactifs.
           Thesis, Université Joseph Fourier, Grenoble, 1990.

[Mil80]   R. Milner. *A Calculus of Communicating Systems, LNCS
           92.* Springer Verlag, 1980.

[Mil83]   R. Milner. Calculi for synchrony and asynchrony. *TCS*,
           25(3), July 1983.

[MM84]   B. Moszkowski and Z. Manna. Reasoning in interval tem-
           poral logic. In *Workshop on Logics of Programs, LNCS
           164.* Springer Verlag, 1984.

[Par92]   J-P. Paris. Exécution de tâches asynchrones depuis Esterel.
           Thesis, University of Nice, 1992.

[PH87]   J. A. Plaice and N. Halbwachs. LUSTRE-V2 user's guide and
           reference manual. Technical Report SPECTRE L2, IMAG,
           Grenoble, October 1987.

[PH88]   D. Pilaud and N. Halbwachs. From a synchronous declar-
           ative language to a temporal logic dealing with multiform
           time. In M. Joseph, editor, *Symposium on Formal Tech-
           niques in Real-Time and Fault-Tolerant Systems, LNCS
           331.* Springer Verlag, September 1988.

[Pla88]   J. A. Plaice. Sémantique et compilation de LUSTRE, un lan-
           gage déclaratif synchrone. Thesis, Institut National Poly-
           technique de Grenoble, 1988.

[Plo81]   G. D. Plotkin. A structural approach to operational seman-
           tics. Lecture notes, Aarhus University, 1981.

[Pnu77]   A. Pnueli. The temporal logic of programs. In *18th Symp.
           on the Foundations of Computer Science.* IEEE, 1977.

[PS87]   J. A. Plaice and J-B. Saint. The LUSTRE-ESTEREL portable
           format.   Unpublished report, INRIA, Sophia Antipolis,
           1987.

[PT87]   R. Paige and R. Tarjan. Three partition refinement algo-
            rithms. *SIAM J. Comput.*, 16(6), 1987.

[QS82]   J. P. Queille and J. Sifakis. Specification and verification of
            concurrent systems in CESAR. In *International Symposium
            on Programming, LNCS 137.* Springer Verlag, April 1982.

[Ray88]   P. Raymond. Compilation séparée de programmes LUSTRE.
            Technical Report SPECTRE L5, IMAG, Grenoble, June
            1988.

[RdS90]   V. Roy and R. de Simone. Auto and Autograph. In R. Kur-
            shan, editor, *International Workshop on Computer Aided
            Verification, Rutgers*, June 1990.

[RH91a]   F. Rocheteau and N. Halbwachs. Implementing reac-
            tive programs on circuits, a hardware implementation of
            LUSTRE. In REX *Workshop on Real-Time: Theory in Prac-
            tice, DePlasmolen (Netherlands), LNCS 600*, pages 195–
            208. Springer Verlag, June 1991.

[RH91b]   F. Rocheteau and N. Halbwachs. POLLUX, a LUSTRE
            based hardware design environment. In P. Quinton and
            Y. Robert, editors, *Conference on Algorithms and Parallel
            VLSI Architectures II, Chateau de Bonas*, June 1991.

[RHR91]   C. Ratel, N. Halbwachs, and P. Raymond. Program-
            ming and verifying critical systems by means of the syn-
            chronous data-flow programming language LUSTRE. In
            *ACM-SIGSOFT'91 Conference on Software for Critical
            Systems*, New Orleans, December 1991.

[Roc89]   F. Rocheteau. Programmation d'un circuit massivement
            parallèle à l'aide d'un langage déclaratif synchrone. Tech-
            nical Report SPECTRE L10, IMAG, Grenoble, June 1989.

[Roy90]   V. Roy. AUTOGRAPH, un outil de visualisation pour les
            calculs de processus. Thesis, University of Nice, 1990.

[RRSV87]   J. L. Richier, C. Rodriguez, J. Sifakis, and J. Voiron. Ver-
            ification in XESAR of the sliding window protocol. In *IFIP
            WG-6.1 7th. International Conference on Protocol Specifi-
            cation, Testing and Verification*. North Holland, 1987.

[RS89]   V. Roy and R. de Simone. An AUTOGRAPH primer. Tech-
            nical Report INRIA, May 1989.

[SP90]   J-B. Saint and J-P. Paris. Les instructions du code in-
            termédiaire, description syntaxique. Unpublished report,
            INRIA, Sophia Antipolis, 1990.

[STB91]   H. Savoj, H. Touati, and R. K. Brayton. The use of im-
            age computation techniques in extracting local don't cares
            and network optimization. In *International Conference on
            Computer Aided Design (ICCAD)*, November 1991.

[Ver86]   D. Vergamini. Verification by means of observational equiv-
            alence on automata. Technical Report 501, INRIA, 1986.

[Xil88]   Xilinx, Inc. The Programmable Gate Array Data Book.
            Product Specification, 1988.

Index